New Nations and Peoples

Israel

Israel

CHAIM BERMANT

with 70 illustrations and 3 maps

WALKER AND COMPANY
NEW YORK

Library of Congress Catalog Card Number: 67–23090

First published in the United States of America in 1967 by Walker and Company, a division of Publications Development Corporation.

Printed in Great Britain by Jarrold and Sons Ltd, Norwich

Contents

1   In the beginning

ISRAEL IS ONE of the youngest states in the world, and is yet among the oldest. Other peoples have recovered their independence after centuries of subjugation, but they existed as a compact entity, living on their own soil, speaking their own language, and enjoying a greater or lesser degree of autonomy. The Jews, on the other hand, had to recover not only their sense of nationhood, but their language, and to transplant themselves physically to a land from which they had been estranged for two thousand years. The history of the Jewish state begins in Europe.

After the destruction of Judea by the Romans in the first century AD, Jews fled in all directions, some eastwards towards the ancient Jewish communities of Babylon, others westwards to Egypt, and from there across the Mediterranean to Spain, Italy and France.

Wherever they settled they usually found themselves under the rule of Rome. They preserved their own way of life, their ritual, their exclusiveness, and the very fact that they were an identifiable minority could on occasion expose them to hostile crowds. Yet on the whole they enjoyed freedom of worship, and even privileges, till the rise of Christianity and its spread from the Mediterranean basin northwards along the Rhône and Rhine.[1]

The first pogroms were perpetrated in France and the Rhineland in 1096 by Crusaders en route for the Holy Land.[2] The Jews were gradually reduced to pariahs, their existence became precarious, and in Christian lands continued to be precarious until comparatively recent times.

They enjoyed greater stability under Islam, and in Moorish Spain in particular there was a rich flowering of Jewish culture, but it was

7

stifled by the Inquisition, and in 1492 the Jews of Spain were expelled.

Throughout the centuries from the fall of Jerusalem until our own times the Jew moved from place to place. Tolerance brought an influx, oppression an exodus. Germany offered a refuge through the very fact that it was a patchwork of petty states, and if the situation became intolerable in one principality it was not difficult to transfer to another. Poland for a time, and especially under Casimir the Great (1333–70), was particularly attractive to the Jew. There was virtually no Polish middle-class, which gave the Jew entrepreneurial openings absent elsewhere. The rulers were tolerant, and at times even benign. Polanyah, the Jews called it in Hebrew, 'Here Dwelleth the Lord'. It was to them what America became to the Jews of the nineteenth century, the golden domain, and a large Jewish settlement grew up.

The incursions of Chmielnicki and his Cossacks, from the Ukrainian territories of the Polish empire, in the seventeenth century, devastated the Jewish community, and the successive partitions of Poland at the end of the eighteenth century placed most of Polish Jewry under Russian rule.

When Theodor Herzl, the Austrian journalist and playwright, launched the Zionist organization in 1897 there were some ten million Jews in the world, of whom nearly half lived in the Tsarist empire. Russia was to be the forcing-house of Zionism.

Throughout his varying change of fortune the Jew maintained an unswerving loyalty to his faith, and among the basic elements of that faith is a belief in the return to Zion. Prayers for the rebuilding of Jerusalem were said, and, paradoxically, still are said, three times a day. They are contained in the grace after meals, and expressions of longing for Zion appear and reappear in the Sabbath and festive liturgy. And the Day of Atonement, the most sacred day in the Jewish year, concludes with the hope of: 'The Next Year in Jerusalem'.

This Zionism was Messianic. The restoration of the Jews to Judea would, it was believed, come about through divine intervention. 'I shall await His coming daily', the Jew would intone with

8

his prayers, and this expressed more than a vague sentiment, so that when self-proclaimed Messiahs appeared, as they did on numerous occasions, Jews in their thousands were ready to forsake all their worldly goods and follow them. To an extent Jewry was thrown into its own inner world by the hostility of the world outside.

The spread of enlightenment in western and central Europe inevitably affected the Jews living there, and Moses Mendelssohn (1729–86), one of the greatest German philosophers of his age, tried to formulate a synthesis which would enable the Jew to divest himself of his particularism without infringing the principles of his faith. He himself translated the Pentateuch (the first five books of the Old Testament) and Psalms into German, and there followed a great effulgence of German-Jewish learning. Mendelssohn's wish to bring *Haskala*, enlightenment, to the Jewish world succeeded too well, but his hope of a synthesis proved too optimistic. German Jews, in the main, once exposed to outside culture rapidly forsook their own.

The Haskala movement did not reach Russia till the nineteenth century. There it assumed a more intrinsically Jewish character, but knowledge of its effects in the West, and the fear that it might do the same in the East, impeded its progress.

The movement flourished on the common optimism of the age. The French Revolution, and the march of Napoleon across Europe, had demolished the walls of the ghettoes. They had not eliminated ancient prejudices, but there remained a faith in progress to which many thinking Jews adhered tenaciously, sometimes in the face of much evidence to the contrary. Between 1840 and the end of the century that faith received three severe, if not fatal, setbacks. The first was the Damascus Blood Libel; the second was a series of pogroms which ravaged the Jewish communities of southern Russia in 1881–2; the third was the arrest and degradation of Alfred Dreyfus.

On 5 February 1840, Father Tomasso, Superior of the Franciscan Convent in Damascus, disappeared without trace. A search began of the Jewish quarter and by means of torture a confession was extorted from a barber that a ritual murder had been planned. As a

9

result seven leading members of the Jewish community were arrested and tortured. One died of his agonies, another sought refuge in Christian baptism. The rest were sentenced to death, but were released after widespread protests in London, Paris and elsewhere.

In medieval Europe Jews had been frequently accused of killing Christians for ritual purposes, and echoes of it were to be heard in Russia as recently as 1911, but it had been unknown in Moslem countries. Syria in 1840, however, was under the rule of Mehemet Ali, a French protégé. The charges of ritual murder had been instigated by local Catholics, and had been supported by the French Consul who, under the Capitulations, directed the trial of the accused.

The event shook the whole of world Jewry and in particular Moses Hess.

Hess (1812–75) was a German Jew, a product of the emancipation movement who, in common with many of his contemporaries, had moved far from his Jewish origins, but who, toward the end of his life, had made a return pilgrimage.

He saw the belief that enlightenment would ameliorate the condition of the Jew and raise him to the level of those about him, as wishful thinking. Legal disabilities might be removed, but social disabilities remained. Such brilliant contemporaries of his as Ludwig Borne and Heinrich Heine (1797–1856) had to become converts to Christianity to open their way to advancement.

Emancipation, wrote Hess in *Rome and Jerusalem*, was alienating the Jew from his heritage without making him acceptable to his neighbours.

'The German hates the Jewish religion no less than the race; he objects less to the Jews' peculiar beliefs than to their peculiar noses.' The Jew, he argued, could be truly emancipated only in his own homeland – this in 1862.

Such arguments hardly affected the great mass of Russian Jewry for the time being. They were largely removed from both the liberal trends in the outside world and the assimilationist trends in the Jewish one. The majority of them continued to live, as they had lived for centuries, on the edge of destitution, subject to almost feudal disabilities, and seeking solace for the harshness of their material environment by an increasing withdrawal into their spiritual one.

About the time that Hess was writing his trenchant analysis of the Jewish question, there appeared another analysis by Zevi Hirsch Kalischer (1795–1874), the celebrated Rabbi of Thorn, East Prussia. Kalischer also felt that the solution to the Jewish problem lay in a Jewish state, but as an Orthodox Rabbi he had to show that this did not have to await the advent of Messiah, and quoted numerous Biblical and Talmudic texts to support his view.[3] He urged that the colonization of Palestine should be undertaken without delay and sought the help of wealthy Jews in the West to finance it. He was a practical visionary and one result of his work was the opening in 1870 of the first Jewish agricultural school in Palestine.

The ideas of Hess and Kalischer led eventually to the formation throughout central and eastern Europe of groups of Chovevei Zion, 'lovers of Zion', but they did not acquire an important following till after the massacres of 1881 and 1882.

Under Alexander II who ascended the throne of Russia in 1855 Russia had entered upon a passing phase of liberalism and some Jews began to feel that their dark age was over. On 13 March 1881, Alexander was assassinated. The reactionaries returned in full force, and their most immediate victims were the Jews. On 27 April a pogrom broke out in the province of Kherson. The disorders spread to Kiev and Odessa in May, and throughout southern Russia in the subsequent summer and autumn. At Christmas there was a violent outbreak in Warsaw. By the end of the year some two hundred Jewish communities had been subjected to murder, arson, pillage and rape. The authorities had done nothing to check the attacks and in some areas were among the attackers.

The Russian Haskala movement which had hoped to raise the Jewish masses in the East to the social and cultural level of their brethren in the West was among the first victims of the pogroms. In 1882 Leo Pinsker, an Odessa physician who had been an advocate of assimilation, published *Auto-Emancipation* to show, as Hess had shown in his own way, that it was a false hope. Antisemitism, he argued, was neither a local nor passing phenomenon, and arose in part out of the very condition of the Jew. He could receive full civic and political rights, yet his emancipation would still be incomplete. The Jew, to have a life of his own, needed a home of his own.

The Chovevei Zion were now growing rapidly throughout Russia and Poland and new groups were formed in Romania and Austria. *Auto-Emancipation* became their Bible, and Pinsker was elected head of the movement. A spearhead of prospective colonists, the Bilu,[4] was formed in Kharkov.

In spite of the terror few Russian Jews thought of Palestine as their refuge. They fled in their tens of thousands in all directions, to America, Britain, South Africa, France, Germany, Austria. In 1882 a handful of Bilu members established Rishon Le Zion, the first permanent Jewish colony in Palestine.

If the assimilationist ideas of an earlier decade hardly touched the Jewish masses in the East the Chovevei Zion hardly affected the Jewish communities in the West. The pogroms struck them as yet further examples of Russian barbarism with which the world had become familiar through the bloody suppression of successive Polish revolts. They were anguished by the sufferings of their brethren, but they looked on what had happened as a purely local, and possibly transitory event. They were confident that their own progress, at least, was assured. It was the Dreyfus Affair which caused rethinking in the West and led to the rise of political Zionism. In 1894 Captain Alfred Dreyfus, a Jew in the French army, was arrested on a charge of treason. As the case developed it became clear that he was innocent and that he was used as a scapegoat to cover the crimes of others.

The Dreyfus Affair was to Theodor Herzl what the Damascus Affair had been to Hess, and the 1881 pogroms to Pinsker.

Herzl (1860–1904) was an urbane, cultivated Viennese Jew, a gifted journalist and literary dilettante who had moved far from his Jewish origins and had little or no contact with organized Jewish life. Antisemitism was rife in Vienna and he had for a while entertained the idea of mass baptism as a solution to it, but he does not appear to have given serious thought to the Jewish problem till the Dreyfus Affair.

Perhaps the most important aspect of the Affair to the Jew was that it happened in France, the home of modern civilization, the harbinger of culture, from which the forces which freed the ghetto Jew first sprang. If France could have such a relapse, could there be emancipation for the Jew anywhere outside a Jewish state? Without having studied Pinsker or Hess, Herzl reached the same conclusion as both of them.

But how was the Jewish state to be created?

The Chovevei Zion indicated one approach. They hoped to form a Jewish society in Palestine by gradual immigration and the establishment of a network of colonies. They had, as we have seen, founded Rishon Le Zion in 1882, and it was followed in rapid succession by Nes Ziona, Zichron Ya'akov, Rosh Pina, Ekron, Gedera, Rehovoth and Hadera. By the end of the century there were 21 Jewish agricultural settlements in Palestine with a population of 3,000.

Herzl, on the other hand, tended to think in terms of massive schemes and grand diplomacy. His *Judenstaat* (Jewish State), published in 1896, advocated a 'Society of Jews' to organize the mass movement of Jews towards their homeland, and a 'Jewish Company' to finance it. He hoped to secure a charter for Palestine from the sultan with the help of funds from Jewish magnates. That particular aspiration proved doubly abortive, for the sultan would not grant a charter, and the magnates did not give the money. The greatest of them all, Baron Edmond de Rothschild, was already pouring billions of francs into the Holy Land, but his approach was paternalistic and he had no faith in Herzl's venture. But the 'Society of Jews' did eventually materialize, and so did the 'Jewish Company'. The first was the Zionist Organization, the second, the Jewish Colonial Trust.

In 1897 the first Zionist Congress assembled in Basle. The transactions of that historic gathering were perhaps less significant than the gathering itself. For the first time in Jewish history representatives from Jewish communities throughout the world had assembled to discuss a programme of action for the Jewish people. 'Zionism, they declared, 'aims at establishing for the Jewish people a publicly and legally assured home in Palestine.' A political movement had come into being and it was Herzl's creation. It was this rather than his frenzied embassies to heads of state which was to earn him the title of 'father of the Jewish state'.

The embassies were, however, necessary, for the Zionist Organization could do little without the patronage of a great power. Herzl had two meetings with the German Kaiser Wilhelm II and they both proved futile. He was, however, able to interest Joseph Chamberlain, the British Colonial Secretary, in the Jewish question, and out of this emerged the East Africa scheme. The British offer of an area of hill country near Nairobi might not in normal circumstances have been seriously considered, but in April 1903 there was a particularly savage pogrom in Kishinev and the question of a secure refuge for the Jew assumed immediate urgency. East Africa was not Palestine, but because of the critical situation of Jewry, Herzl favoured acceptance. His very readiness to do so showed how far he was removed from the feelings which gave Zionism its main impetus. He found influential supporters for the scheme, but the mass of the movement opposed it on the sufficient grounds that there could be no Zionism without Zion. But the scheme, while causing division and bitterness in the movement, had one important positive result. A great power had concerned herself with the work of the Zionist movement. Zionism had found, if not a patron, at least a sympathetic listener.

Among the opponents of the East Africa scheme was Chaim Weizmann, then in his late twenties.

Weizmann was born in Motol, near Pinsk, in 1873 and became active in the Chovevei Zion movement while still at school. He was a student in Berlin when the *Judenstaat* was published. None of its propositions was new, but Weizmann, like other members of the Zionist student movement, was roused by the sense of urgency in the pamphlet. It was the work of a man of action.

Yet much as he admired Herzl, Weizmann had critical reservations about his attitudes. He did not share his belief in Jewish magnates, in the great powers, or that a Jewish state could be brought into being by the flourish of a pen. 'To me', he wrote, 'Zionism was something organic, which had to grow like a plant, had to be watched, watered and nursed, if it was to reach maturity.'[5]

It was natural when the division came in the Zionist movement on the East Africa scheme that he should be among its opponents. Yet, although he distrusted charters and dramatic flourishes and believed, so to speak, in the inevitability of gradualness, he more than any man was responsible for the most dramatic gesture in Zionist history, the Balfour Declaration.

In 1904 he came to England to take up a post in biochemistry at Manchester University and rapidly built up an influential circle of friends and acquaintances, including C. P. Scott of the *Manchester Guardian*, through whom he met Lloyd George and Herbert Samuel.

During the war he was seconded to the Admiralty and there was instrumental in perfecting a new process for the manufacture of acetone. His discovery was of crucial importance to the war effort and Lloyd George suggests in his *War Memoirs*[6] that the Balfour Declaration was a reward for his services. 'I almost wish it had been as simple as that', Weizmann commented later.[7]

Many reasons have been given for the Balfour Declaration, the most common being that the British government was anxious to win the support of American Jewry, and hence America, at a critical stage in the war, or that it was made to forestall a similar declaration by Germany. Herbert Samuel had also argued that a Jewish state in Palestine was in Britain's strategic interest. The Jews of eastern Europe were shattered by the backward and forward movement of the Russian, the Austro-Hungarian and the German armies, and there was much sympathy for their suffering. There were also a number of genuine Zionist sympathizers in the administration, most notably the Foreign Secretary, Arthur Balfour, whom Weizmann had met in 1906. In the final analysis the Declaration was a combination of idealism and self-interest, with the latter possibly predominating.[8]

On 2 November 1917, Balfour wrote to Lord Rothschild:

His Majesty's government view with favour the establishment in Palestine of a national home for the Jewish people, and will use their best endeavours to facilitate the achievement of this object, it being clearly understood that nothing shall be done which may prejudice the civil and religious rights of existing non-Jewish communities in Palestine, or the rights and political status enjoyed by Jews in any other country.

Zionism had won its charter. But it was only the beginning.

2　　The five waves

THE ROMANS WHO DID EVERYTHING to suppress Jewish life in Judea did not entirely extirpate its inhabitants. The country was devastated, Jerusalem was in ruins, but the Jews somehow contrived to maintain a corporate existence, and even to multiply.

When the Arabs under the Caliph Omar occupied Palestine in AD 637 there were said to have been between 300,000 and 400,000 Jews in the country. Their numbers dwindled as a result of the succeeding wars, the Crusades, and the Mongol invasion. By the end of the last century when the first of the Bilu pioneers settled in Palestine, there were 24,000 Jews in Palestine, half of them in Jerusalem, the rest in Safad, Tiberias and Hebron.

These inhabitants were generally referred to as the old Yishuv, or the old settlement, as distinct from the new which was about to descend.

The old Yishuv consisted almost entirely of pious Jews and their families who spent their days largely in devotional studies, and depended for their livelihood on emissaries who toured the Jewish communities of Europe collecting funds. The apportionment of this fund was known as the *Haluka*. It allowed them a bare existence but as long as they were able to continue their studies they needed nothing more. They were entirely unworldly and apolitical, and sought no share in the affairs of the new Yishuv.

The term Haluka, with its connotations of dependence and subordination, came to represent all that the new Yishuv despised in the old, but the new was never entirely free from the Haluka itself and there are Israelis today who look upon the dispatch of Ministers to solicit funds from diaspora Jewry as a perpetuation of the same principle.

Some 450,000 Jews settled in Palestine between 1882 and the outbreak of the Second World War in 1939. They came in five main waves each of which is referred to as an *Aliya*, and each of which differed considerably in size and character from the other.

The First Aliya, consisting of some 25,000 immigrants, came in the years 1882–1903. They were the products of the Chovevei Zion and varied in age and background. They were nearly all from the cities and towns of Russia and Romania, and without agricultural experience or any idea of the special difficulties they would meet in squeezing a livelihood from the stony soil of Palestine. They showed determination, zeal and incredible hardihood, but these attributes were not sufficient and, but for the generous subsidies of Baron Edmond de Rothschild, the colonies which they established would almost certainly have collapsed.

The same Rothschild, we may recall, was not impressed by Herzl's political ideas, but after his first visit to Palestine in 1887 he was deeply moved by what the new settlers were trying to do, and from then on he poured millions of pounds into the country.

Among the colonies thus helped were Petach Tikva, Rishon Le Zion, Zichron Ya'akov, Rosh Pina, Yesod Hama'ala, Nes Ziona, Mishmar Hayarden and Gedera. In 1890 two colonies were established without the aid of Rothschild. They were Rehovoth and Hadera.

Although the settlers toiled tirelessly they saw no need to dispense with the labour of others, and in this they differed fundamentally from the communal and collective settlements founded by members of the Second and Third Aliya. They had become farmers and small-holders and as Arab labour was abundant and cheap their employees were mostly Arabs. The exceptions were the wine-cellars of Rishon Le Zion and Zichron Ya'akov where for religious reasons only Jews could be employed.

The First Aliya for all its self-sacrifice and zeal was thus per-petuating the old order rather than creating a new one. It was in its homeland rather than exile, rural rather than urban, agrarian rather than entrepreneurial, but still *petit bourgeois* and in many ways still transmitting the values of the society it had abandoned.

The Second Aliya began in 1904, a year after the Kishinev pogrom in which 45 Jews lost their lives, a year after the outbreak of the Russo-Japanese war, and a year before the failure of the 1905 Russian revolution. All three events helped to speed the flow of immigrants who by 1914 totalled 40,000. They were in the main working-class, with a rich sprinkling of intellectuals dispirited by the collapse of the revolution.

Among their mentors was A. D. Gordon, a follower of Tolstoy, a member of a prosperous Russian-Jewish family, who at the age of 48 settled in Palestine to till the soil, an activity totally alien to him and to the vast majority of Jews of his class. He believed in the inherent nobility of labour and his belief took root.

At the Fifth Zionist Congress in 1901 the Jewish National Fund was established to acquire land in Palestine for Jewish settlement. A Palestine Office under Dr Arthur Ruppin was opened in Jaffa and in 1908 land was bought round the southern shore of the Sea of Galilee and in the Valley of Jezreel. Both were marshy and inhospitable, but they provided much-needed employment for the new immigrants from Russia.

If convinced of the dignity of labour the newcomers were not always convinced that there was any dignity in the role of the hired labourer and friction developed between them and their overseers. In 1909 a handful of them undertook the cultivation of a 75-acre area near Tiberias, without overseers, and did so efficiently and profitably. They had undertaken the work only as a gesture and after proving their point they moved elsewhere. They were replaced by a group of 10 men and 2 women, who remained on the site permanently and called it Degania. They had started with no set plan to conduct a social experiment, but out of their experience grew the institution which was to form the backbone of the Jewish state – the *kibbutz*.

Many members of the Second Aliya came imbued with socialist ideas, but the form of the kibbutz was to a large extent determined by their circumstances. If they hoped to remain economically viable and continue without external interference, and defend themselves against marauders, this could best be done on a collective basis.

The kibbutzim embody the principle: from each according to his ability, to each according to his needs. No wages are paid and all work, property and amenities are shared, though, perhaps unavoidably, the veteran is more comfortably housed than the newcomer. They are administered by an elected secretariat, and the highest authority of the kibbutz is the general meeting of members. They are basically agricultural enterprises, but many kibbutzim have profitable factories, workshops and guest-houses.

The success of Degania encouraged the Palestine Office to establish other collective settlements near by and in the Jezreel valley, but it should not be thought that the Second or any other Aliya consisted entirely or even largely of prospective kibbutzniks. They were nearly all townsmen, and most of them made for the towns and stayed there. Jerusalem expanded, Haifa grew and in 1908 Tel-Aviv was founded as a suburb of Jaffa.

The old Yishuv, a considerable part of it still subsisting on Haluka, continued to form a substantial part of the population. The idealism which had propelled the early Bilu pioneers was wearing thin, and their children who were growing to maturity did not always care to carry on the work of their fathers. Many of them drifted into the towns or out of the country, but with all the local setbacks there was no gainsaying the progress which had been made on the broad front. By 1914 there were 43 Jewish rural settlements in Palestine with a population of nearly 8,000, firmly rooted, productive, many of them with their own defence units. And in the country as a whole there were 85,000 Jews forming $12\frac{1}{2}$ per cent of the population. No important political advance had been made outside, no charter gained. Palestine was still a remote and misgoverned province of the Ottoman empire, its population still overwhelmingly Arab, but there was already stirring within it the beginnings of a Jewish state.

Then came the war. Turkey and Russia were on opposite sides, and most of the newcomers were Russian. The Turkish authorities issued a decree against 'the subversive element aiming at the creation of a Jewish government in the Palestinian part of the Ottoman empire'. The Anglo-Palestine Bank, an offshoot of the Jewish Colonial Trust, the financial arm of the Zionist Organization, founded in 1903, was closed. The use of Hebrew on public signs was banned.[9] The settlers' defence organization, *Hashomer*, was proscribed. All subjects of the Allied Powers were given a choice between deportation and enrolment in the Turkish army. Added to this were the hardships arising from war and blockade, and it was only the prompt and generous intervention of American Jewry which saved what was left of the Yishuv from starvation.

The outbreak of war left the Zionist movement in a quandary, for its leaders and rank and file were scattered among both the Central Powers and the Allies.

Weizmann, an inveterate anglophile, had, as we have seen, thrown in his lot with the Allies, and several of his colleagues, while not wholly sharing his pro-British passions, were convinced that Britain would win. Among them were Vladimir Jabotinsky and Josef Trumpeldor.

The former was a brilliant journalist and orator, a fiery, controversial figure, who was later to break away from the Zionist movement and form a more militant organization of his own. The latter was a hero of the Russo-Japanese war, the first Jew to hold commissioned rank in the Russian army. Both found themselves in Alexandria at the outbreak of war, and there they conceived the idea of a Jewish Battalion to fight in the Allied cause. Out of this grew the Jewish Legion which was not finally formed until 1917, and which saw little action, but it had immense psychological value for the Zionists. For the first time since the revolt of Bar Kochba against Rome in the second century, Jews had borne arms as Jews.

Among the members of the Legion were David Ben Gurion and Itzhak Ben Zvi, the first Prime Minister and the second President of Israel respectively, and Eliahu Golomb, Dov Hos and Ya'akov Dori, who were among the architects of the Hagana, Israel's future army.[10]

During the war years the fortunes of the Zionist movement were transformed. On the positive side was the Balfour Declaration. On the negative side the three million Jews of Russia, who had formed the mass following of the Zionist movement, from which the First

and Second Aliya had been mainly recruited, and which had provided a substantial portion of Zionist funds, had been removed from
Zionism by the Bolshevik revolution. Jews for a time were allowed
to leave Russia, but no Jew in Russia could further the Zionist cause.

Poland, the Baltic states, Romania, Hungary, Austria, Germany
were in turmoil, but Zionist work continued apace. The Twelfth
Zionist Congress, which met in September 1921, represented
770,000 members compared with 129,400 in 1913.

The delegates were divided into three main groups which continue to function till our own day: the General Zionists 306, the
Mizrachi (religious Zionists) 97, and Labour 38.[11]

A year earlier, in 1920, the Zionist Organization had launched
the Keren Hayesod to finance the movement and absorption of
immigrants. It was intended as a voluntary tithe upon the members
of the organization, and it was hoped to raise £25,000,000 a year.
In the event it yielded about £600,000 in the first 18 months and
ambitious projects had to be reduced or shelved.[12]

This affected the fortunes of the Third Aliya whose members
began arriving in 1920 at the rate of about 10,000 a year. Many of
them were young people who had been fired by the example of
Degania and other collective settlements, but they could at first only
find work on public works projects. In 1921, however, a further
stretch of the Valley of Jezreel – 17,500 acres in all – was acquired
by the Jewish National Fund, and in that year kibbutz Ein Harod
was founded.

That year also saw the formation of the first *moshav*. (In the latter,
as distinct from the former, each member works a plot of his own,
and pockets any surplus which he may earn. Most buying and
selling is conducted on a cooperative basis, and all machinery is
communally owned.)

Under Ottoman rule Palestinian manufactures largely consisted
of wine, soap, olive-wood articles and religious appurtenances. New
industries were now developed. In 1921 an electric power station
was built in Tel-Aviv, a salt plant in Atlit in 1922 and flour and
oil mills in Haifa in 1923. In 1925 a cement industry was
established.

At the end of the war the population of the Yishuv had shrunk to 55,000. By 1925 this number had doubled. The population of Haifa had grown from 2,000 to 8,000, that of Tel-Aviv from 2,000 to 30,000. The administration of Palestine was taken over from the Ottoman empire by Britain which, in due course, was vested with a mandate over the country by the League of Nations.

The Yishuv was allowed to choose its own elected assembly, the Assephat Hanivcharim, which in turn elected a national council, the Vaad Leumi, and gradually the development of Jewish Palestine became a partnership between the Vaad Leumi inside the country, and the Zionist movement outside.

In a White Paper as early as 1921, Britain noted that the Yishuv:

has its own political organs; an elected assembly for the direction of its domestic organisation and for the control of its schools. It has an elected Chief Rabbi and Rabbinical Council for the direction of its religious affairs. Its business is conducted in Hebrew as the vernacular language, and a Hebrew press serves its needs. It has its distinctive intellectual life and displays considerable economic activity. This community, then, with its town and country population, its political, religious, social organisation, its own language, its own customs, its own life, has in fact 'national' characteristics.[13]

The Fourth Aliya, which began in 1924, brought a flow of middle-class people with middle-class sympathies and some capital, and over 80,000 of them settled in the country by 1932. They moved mainly to the large towns, but new settlements on private land, financed by private capital, grew up, including Bnei Brak, Magdiel, Herzliya, Ramatayim and Kfar Ata.

From 1924 to 1926 the country enjoyed an immense building boom, but as the boom spent itself, employment declined. Most of the newcomers were from Poland and the collapse of the Polish economy in 1926 affected their enterprises. Depression set in. In 1927 there were 13,400 Jews out of work. In that year some 2,000 Jews entered the country and over 5,000 left.

The turning point came at the end of 1928. In the following year, while the rest of the world tottered on the brink of depression, Palestine entered upon another boom.

In 1929 the country was shattered by a series of anti-Jewish outbreaks. There had been trouble before. In March 1920 there was an Arab attack on Metulla and Tel-Hai in the extreme north of the country. Josef Trumpeldor and 6 other defenders were killed and the outposts had to be evacuated. In April there were anti-Jewish riots in the Old City of Jerusalem in which 6 Jews were killed and more than 200 wounded. Violence broke out anew twelve months later, this time in Jaffa, in which 47 Jews and 48 Arabs lost their lives. But nothing that had happened previously could compare to the ferocity and scale of the 1929 disorders.

The worst incidents took place in Hebron, where in one particularly brutal attack 59 Jewish men, women and children were butchered. There was a vicious onslaught on the Jews of Safad. Villages in Galilee, the hill country of Jerusalem, the Judean foot-hills and in southern Judea were razed. In one week 105 Jews perished and a further 185 were wounded.

There followed a Commission of Inquiry as a result of which the British government issued a White Paper which would have virtually brought a halt to further Zionist development in Palestine.

The Paper marked a watershed in Anglo-Zionist relations. The Zionist Organization had not always been happy with the way the British government interpreted its obligations under the Balfour Declaration, but it had always been assumed that the Declaration was a fundamental article of policy. The 1930 White Paper was almost a counter-declaration.

To the Jews this seemed to be the reward for the restraint they had shown during the outbreaks, and both the Yishuv and Jewry outside were overcome by a deep feeling of disillusionment about the good faith of Britain. The British government, however, later published a reinterpretation of the White Paper which altered the character of those parts of it to which the Jews had taken particular exception. Immigration, which had been suspended for a time, was again resumed.

Up to 1933 the flow of immigrants stemmed overwhelmingly from eastern Europe, but among them were the occasional idealists or far-sighted individuals from Germany or Austria.

In 1933 Hitler came to power, and thereafter the Jews from Germany and central Europe arrived in a torrent. This was the beginning of the Fifth Aliya.

This new wave of arrivals differed in several respects from their predecessors.

The Jews of the German-speaking lands had been among the first to be emancipated, and in spite of the endemic antisemitism all about them they had advanced in the arts, in politics, in commerce, in almost every field of endeavour, to the forefront of national life. Many were so assimilated that they were recognized as Jews only by anti-semites, but even those who maintained their Jewish identity liked to think of themselves as Germans of the Mosaic persuasion, and were intensely proud of their Germanic culture.

When, after 1933, they were compelled to uproot themselves, those who settled in Palestine brought their German culture with them. They were slow to acquire Hebrew, or did not acquire it at all, and a German-language press grew up to serve them. New banks and trading concerns sprang up. German became the language of commerce. There was a great inflow of doctors, lawyers, artists, musicians. Life in Palestine, in spite of the tragedy which lay behind the Fifth Aliya, became more urbane. The cities acquired a decidedly European aspect, with wide boulevards, ornate cafés and all the amenities of modern living.

The new wave of immigrants was more prosperous than the old. This helped to speed their flow. From 1922 to 1937 the criterion for the admission of immigrants was the 'economic capacity of the country at the time to absorb new arrivals'.[14] There was thus no impediment to the immigrant with capital. In 1930 there were 178 Jewish immigrants with at least £1,000 to their name. Their number rose to 727 in 1932, 3,250 in 1933, and 6,309 in 1935.

In the twenty years 1919–39 about £120,000,000 in Jewish capital was brought into the country, more than a third of it arriving in the last four.

In 1929 Chaim Weizmann had succeeded in widening the basis of the Jewish Agency by bringing in leading non-Zionist Jews from America and Britain, and through them he was able to attract more capital. The pace of development quickened. The settlements destroyed in the 1929 riots were rebuilt.

New towns sprang up: Nahariah, a European-style watering resort to the north of Haifa; Ramath-Hashauim; Kiryat Bialik, all of them peopled by new immigrants from Germany. Natanya to the north of Tel-Aviv was founded as a new industrial centre. Haifa harbour was completed in 1933, and in 1934 the Kirkuk–Haifa pipe-line of the Iraq Petroleum Company began to flow.

In the rift valley of the Arava a large chemical industry was established to exploit the mineral deposits of the Dead Sea. The Jewish acreage under citrus grew from 15,000 in 1930 to 40,000 in 1936. Between 1932 and 1936, 17 new agricultural settlements were established. Government revenue which had been two and a half million Palestine pounds in 1930 approached £P6,000,000 in 1935–6. Exports rose from £P2,078,000 in 1930 to £P4,267,000 in 1936. The Administration, which had been empowered to raise a £P2,000,000 loan for various agricultural improvements and public works, was able to pay for them from current revenue.[15] The economy was booming, the prosperity was unprecedented. And the Arabs shared in it all, through new outlets for their labour, as with the Palestine Potash Company, or through the growing demand for their goods and services. The Arab birth-rate soared and death-rate fell, and the Arab population grew from 660,000 in 1922 to 860,000 in 1932, and to nearly a million five years later.

'Everyone in Palestine agrees that the economic development is astonishing,' wrote Sir Herbert Samuel, a former High Commissioner of the country, 'no one thinks that the political situation shows any appreciable improvement.'[16]

And the political situation, which had never been entirely stable, began to deteriorate even amidst the prosperity. The Arabs had replied to the resumption of Jewish immigration in 1932 with an economic boycott and an outbreak of lawlessness which the British administration, however, had no difficulty in suppressing.

In 1936 there were further outbreaks which rapidly grew into a full-scale rebellion.

Yet another Commission of Inquiry was sent out and it found, what had been obvious to many observers for some time, that the Mandate which had been entrusted to Britain by the Council of the League of Nations in 1920 was not working and could not be made to work. The aspirations of Jews and Arabs were irreconcilable, and the only solution was partition.

1 Relics of the Roman Empire which destroyed most of the Judaea (part of which Israel now constitutes), the home of the Jewish people for centuries, in the first century AD. Dating from this period is this magnificent red porphyry at Caesarea which was once part of a large public building adorned with statues and marble columns.

2 After the destruction of Jerusalem in 70 AD the Jews preserved their exclusiveness and, more important, their religion. These remains of a restored Hellenistic synagogue of Kfar Bira'm was probably built during this period.

3 The Jews in the course of their wandering were exposed to great hostility and unjust accusations, the worst of which was the notorious blood libel. According to this engraving, made in the fifteenth century and entitled 'Ritual murder at Trent', Jews were said to sacrifice Christian children so that their blood might be used for the production of unleavened bread eaten at the Jewish Passover.

4 A Jewish moneylender and a German peasant from a sixteenth-century woodcut. Moneylending was virtually the sole occupation in which Jews could engage for they were excluded from almost everything else by the trade and merchant guilds.

5 The Christian Lateran Councils of the twelfth century enforced anti-Jewish legislation. In particular Jews were made to wear distinctive badges and pointed hats thus setting them apart from their so-called Christian neighbours.

6 The Spanish Inquisition of the fifteenth century caused the exile of thousands of Jews to North Africa. This nineteenth-century drawing shows a young Jewish girl.

7 Moroccan Jews at a Jewish wedding feast.

8 Moses Mendelssohn (1729–86) was the founder of the Haskala (enlightenment) movement which sought to eliminate Jewish particularism without infringing religious faith.

9 *(below left)* Theodor Herzl (1860–1904) was the founder of political Zionism and the prophet of the Jewish state.

10 *(below right)* Moses Hess (1812–75), a German Jew, was the progenitor of the idea that the Jew could only be truly emancipated in his homeland.

11 Antisemitism in the nineteenth century reached a climax with the trial of a Jewish staff officer, Captain Alfred Dreyfus, who was charged with treason.

12 (*left below*) Lord Lionel de Rothschild (1808–79), the head of the English branch of the family who had made substantial financial contributions to the establishment of the Jewish state.

13 (*right below*) Alfred James Balfour (1840–1930) issued the declaration which was to form the Charter of the Jewish state.

14 (*left above*) The Zionist
Commission which had been
sent to Palestine by the British
Government in 1918 to survey
the situation on behalf of all
Jewry.

15 (*left below*) Under the
British Mandate (1920–48)
clashes between Arab and Jew
reached a climax in the 1929
Hebron riots when this
photograph of Jewish vehicles
under British guard was taken.

16 (*right above*) Armed
conflict between Arab
and Jews worsened during the
years prior to 1948. The
United Nations appointed
Count Falk Bernadotte (*right*)
as mediator who made
abortive efforts for truce and
cease fire.

17 (*right below*) Chaim
Weizmann (1874–1952)
was the progenitor of the
1917 Balfour Declaration and
the first President of the state of
Israel. Here he is seen with
with President Truman in
1948. It had long been US
policy to support the
establishment of Israel.

18 The advent of Hitler in 1933 precipitated a series of events which led to the mass murder of millions of Jews and greatly increased the need for a Jewish home where thousands could seek refuge.

19 Auschwitz was one of the concentration camps to which these innocent victims were taken.

3   The clash of nationalisms

ZIONISM WAS, IN PART, an outgrowth of European national/
ism. And that same nationalism which in the course of the nineteenth
century deprived the Ottoman empire of her European possessions,
began, in time, to infect her Arab territories.

The Arabs, unlike the Jews, were on their own lands, but like
them they needed the support of a great power, and early in 1914
Hussein, Sharif of Mecca, approached the British High Com/
missioner in Egypt, Sir Henry MacMahon, to see what support he
would receive in a revolt against the sultan. His approach was a
little premature, for the preservation of the integrity of the Ottoman
empire had been a basic element of British foreign policy since the
time of Pitt. At the end of the year, however, Turkey entered the
war on the side of the Central Powers, and early in 1915 Sir Henry
resumed the negotiations with Hussein.

Hussein was ruler of the most backward part of the Ottoman
empire, but as Sharif of Mecca and custodian of Islam's most sacred
shrine he enjoyed vast prestige in the Arab world and as such
could prove to be an important rallying point against the sultan,
Abdul Hamid.

As the price of the revolt Hussein sought dominion over almost
the entire Arabian peninsula, Iraq, Palestine, Transjordan and
Syria.

Sir Henry, in a letter dated 25 October 1915, made reservations
about the districts of Mersina and Alexandretta, 'and portions of
Syria lying to the west of the districts of Damascus, Homs, Hama
and Aleppo cannot be said to be purely Arab. . . '.[17]

Subject to these reservations Sir Henry confirmed that Britain was prepared 'to recognize and support the independence of the Arabs in all the regions within the limits demanded by the Sharif of Mecca'.

On 5 June 1916, the revolt began.

Sir Henry subsequently maintained that the correspondence did not include Palestine, and the Colonial Office argued, a little disingenuously, that the references to the 'portions of Syria lying to the west of the districts of Damascus, Homs, Hama and Aleppo' also included Palestine, which is indeed to the west of Damascus, but much as Devon is to the west of Newcastle. To that extent the MacMahon letter was in conflict with the Balfour Declaration.

It was also in conflict with a secret pact signed between Britain and France, known from the names of the signatories as the Sykes-Picot agreement, which apportioned the area into British and French zones, and British and French spheres of influence, with Palestine to be 'subjected to a special régime to be determined by agreement between Russia, Britain and France'.

The Bolsheviks revealed the details of the pact in 1917 and an Anglo-French statement of war aims was therefore issued which promised 'administrations deriving their authority from the initiative and free choice of the indigenous populations'. Palestine was not mentioned.

The leadership of the Zionist movement had in the meantime devolved upon Chaim Weizmann and in January 1919 he had a meeting on the future of Palestine with the Emir Feisal, a son of Hussein, and they agreed that:

> All necessary measures shall be taken to encourage and stimulate immigration of Jews into Palestine on a large scale. . . . In taking such measures the Arab peasant and tenant farmers shall be protected in their rights, and shall be assisted in forwarding their economic development.[18]

While the dismemberment of the Turkish empire was being considered at the Peace Conference there seemed a reasonable hope that Arab and Jewish aspirations might be reconciled, but Feisal based his agreement with Weizmann on the satisfaction of his claims elsewhere, and these were frustrated.

At San Remo, in April 1920, the Council of the League of Nations entrusted Britain with the Mandate for Palestine, which embodied the provisions of the Balfour Declaration.

Under Article IV of the Mandate a Jewish Agency was created 'for the purpose of advising and cooperating with the Administration of Palestine in such economic, social and other matters as may affect the establishment of the Jewish national home . . .'. The Zionist Organization was recognized as this agency, and Chaim Weizmann, as President of the Zionist Organization, became its head.

Britain also hoped to create an Arab Agency, but this, like many similar proposals, met with a blank wall of refusal. The Arabs, though divided on many issues, were united in their opposition to the Mandate, and they wished to make no gesture which might suggest that their opposition was weakening. They looked on the Jew as an alien intruder, and the threat of Jewish domination enabled Moslem and Christian Arabs, who had been bitter enemies under the Turks, to compose their differences. In 1920 they formed the Palestine Arab Congress whose Executive acted as spokesman of the Arab population.

From 1918 to 1920 Palestine remained under British military rule, and the local commanders tended on the whole to favour the Arab population more than the Jewish newcomers. The civilian administration which took over in 1920 was also similarly disposed.

A Zionist Commission under Chaim Weizmann had been sent out to Palestine in 1918 to act as intermediary between the British authorities and the Jewish population and to direct the work of relief and rehabilitation. Its efforts were hampered by the authorities and Weizmann had on occasion to protest to London over the heads of the men on the spot. The pattern of the future relationship between the Zionists and the administration was already discernible, and it encouraged the Arabs in their intransigence.

In 1920 the hopes of the Jews were raised by the appointment of Sir Herbert Samuel as the first High Commissioner. Sir Herbert, unlike most English Jews of his class, was both a practising member of his faith and a Zionist sympathizer.

In August, on the Sabbath following the Fast of Ab, which commemorates the destruction of the Temple and the beginning of Jewish exile, he walked from Government House to the Churban Synagogue in the Old City of Jerusalem, and there, in keeping with the tradition of that day, read from the Book of Isaiah:

> Comfort ye, comfort ye my people, saith your God. Speak ye comfortably to Jerusalem, and cry unto her that her warfare is accomplished.

The hour of redemption seemed to be at hand. In September the first Immigration Ordinance was enacted and Samuel authorized the admission of 16,500 Jews.

The Arabs were alarmed by the ordinance, as they were disturbed by the whole direction of British policy. The *effendi* class in particular was concerned lest its privileges be affected by the social changes accompanying this Jewish influx.

When riots broke out in May 1921 martial law was declared and Jewish immigration was suspended. A Commission of Inquiry found that the Arabs were 'generally the aggressors', and the Arab hostility was 'connected with Jewish immigration and with their conception of Zionist policy as derived from Jewish exponents'.

On 3 June 1922, Mr Winston Churchill, who was then Colonial Secretary, issued a more precise definition of the Balfour Declaration which stressed that Palestine as a whole was not to be a Jewish national home, but that such a home was to be founded in Palestine, and that to this end 'the Jewish Community in Palestine should be able to increase its numbers by immigration, it being understood that such immigration should not exceed . . . the economic capacity of the country, that the immigrants should not be a burden on the people of Palestine as a whole and that they should not deprive any section of the population of their employment'.[19]

At the same time he excised the area of Palestine to the east of the Jordan and placed it under the dominion of the Emir Abdullah, a brother of Feisal.

The partition did not seriously disturb Zionist leaders. The historical claim of Jewry to Transjordan was tenuous, and the Jewish settlements were all on the west bank. What was disturbing was the redefinition of the Balfour Declaration, for there was all the difference in the world between Palestine as a Jewish home and a Jewish home in Palestine. But the position of the Jews in eastern Europe, harassed by a rampant nationalism, was critical. And London, partly through the efforts of the Northcliffe press, was passing through one of its more anti-Zionist phases. Churchill's offer, in the circumstances, was the best that could be hoped for, and the Zionists accepted with reluctance. The Arabs were under no such pressure to cooperate.

In 1922 Sir Herbert Samuel, as a step towards self-government, proposed to set up a Legislative Council composed of the High Commissioner, ten official members, and twelve elected members, of whom ten were to be Arabs, and two Jews. The Arabs insisted on an overall majority, and when they could not get their way, boycotted the Council. When Sir Herbert reverted to an Advisory Council, they boycotted that too.

In 1925 Sir Herbert was succeeded as High Commissioner by Field-Marshal Lord Plumer.

The hopes which Samuel's appointment had raised in Jewish breasts were bound to be disappointed. The Jewish population of Palestine and the area of land in Jewish ownership had been doubled during his years of office, but the Zionists felt that in his anxiety to be fair to the Arabs, he had sometimes been unfair to the Jews. One particular act for which he was frequently reproached later was the appointment of Haj Amin al Husseini as Mufti of Jerusalem.

Husseini, scion of one of Palestine's most eminent Arab families, was sentenced *in absentia* to ten years imprisonment for his part in the 1920 riots. He was amnestied shortly after and appointed Mufti, in the hope that he might be tamed and made cooperative by office. In the event he became the most implacable foe of both the Jews and Britain.

As Mufti he became President of the Supreme Moslem Council, a body which enjoyed considerable power through its control of the Moslem religious courts, and the large funds accruing from religious endowments, and, until he fled the country in 1937, he used the Council to foment strife, and as a spearhead of Palestine Arab nationalism.

The middle twenties were, by Palestinian standards, tranquil years.

In spite of the lack of political cooperation, there was considerable cooperation in the social and economic spheres, and in 1926 the administration felt so encouraged by the appearance of amity as to reduce the armed forces of the country to one RAF squadron and two companies of armoured cars. The police were likewise reorganized and reduced.

The severe economic depression of the years 1926–8 kept down the level of immigration and this may have helped to keep the peace. The firm administration of the High Commissioner, FieldMarshal Lord Plumer, certainly did. He was replaced by Sir John Chancellor who was somewhat less firm.

In 1929 the Jewish Agency was reorganized. Under the terms of the Mandate the Zionist Organization, while recognized as the Agency, was required 'to secure the cooperation of all Jews who are willing to assist in the establishment of the Jewish National Home'.[20]

This provision was the subject of fierce controversy at successive Zionist congresses.

Congress is the supreme authority of the Zionist movement and consists of several hundred delegates elected by members of the movement on a party basis. It normally meets every two years and elects a General Council of several score members, and an Executive. The latter has always been a coalition of representatives of all parties according to their strength in Congress.

Until 1931 the majority of delegates were General Zionists who, as their name implied, did not adhere to any particular party creed. In 1925 Vladimir Jabotinsky formed a new party, the Revisionists, who wanted a return to Herzl's concept of Zionism and demanded a Jewish state on both sides of the Jordan; and the Revisionists were fiercely opposed to the inclusion of nonZionist Jews, however eminent, in the Jewish Agency.

Weizmann, however, was able to overcome their opposition, and his plans for an enlarged Jewish Agency were approved by the 1929 Congress. It provided for a Council of 200 members and an Administrative Committee of 40, which was roughly equivalent to the General Council of the Zionist Organization. Weizmann was elected President of the Jewish Agency; Louis Marshall, founder and President of the American Jewish Committee, was elected Chairman of the Council; and Lord Melchett, Chairman of Imperial Chemical Industries, Associate-Chairman. Felix Warburg, the banker, was elected Chairman of the Administrative Committee.

The first meeting of the new Council was an historic occasion, attended by some of the greatest Jewish figures of the day, including Albert Einstein, Sir Herbert Samuel and Léon Blum. It was a demonstration of solidarity and the association of figures like Melchett and Warburg with Zionism helped the flow of new investments to Palestine, but it was not a lasting arrangement. The Zionists always maintained control of the enlarged body, and the non-Zionists fell away, so that to all intents and purposes the Zionist Organization and the Jewish Agency have always been one and the same.

And even the joy which attended the formation of the enlarged body was short-lived, for a few days after the historic Council meeting, details of the 1929 riots and the Hebron massacre burst upon the world.

They had been sparked off by a small incident which itself epitomized the tensions between Jews and Arabs.[21]

The most sacred shrine in Judaism, the Wailing Wall, a remnant of Herod's temple, is an outer wall of the Moslem shrine, the Haram al-Sharif.

Normally it was used only by a few devout Jews, but on fast days it was crowded with worshippers, including women.

In 1928, on the eve of the Day of Atonement, a number of Jews, in accordance with Orthodox practice, put up a temporary screen to separate the males from the females. Moslems complained that it was a breach of the *status quo*, and the screen was removed by a British police officer while prayers were in progress.

The Moslems, led by the Mufti, now began to suggest that the Jews had designs on their holy places. They were unwittingly helped by a number of youngsters from *Bethar*, the youth movement of the extremist Revisionist party, who, on the Fast of Ab on 15 August 1929, held a demonstration at the Wall, demanding that it be placed under Jewish control and swearing to defend it. The next day Moslems invaded the Wall area, but were checked by the police. The police were too few to check the succession of incidents which followed, and within a week the whole country was aflame. Reinforcements were rushed in from Egypt and Malta, and the inevitable Commission of Inquiry, this time under Sir Walter Shaw, a former Chief Justice of the Straits Settlements, was sent out.

The Commission found that the outbreak was 'neither provoked, premeditated nor directed against the British administration', but that it 'was from the beginning an attack by Arabs on Jews, for which no excuse in the form of earlier murders by Jews had been established'. The Mufti was blamed for having a share in the disturbances, but their root cause, said the Commission, lay in the Arabs' 'disappointment of their political and national aspirations and fear for their economic future'.[22]

The British government now dispatched Sir John Hope Simpson, formerly of the Indian Civil Service, to see how far the economic future of the Arabs was affected by Jewish immigration, and to inquire into the absorptive capacity of Palestine.

His report was accompanied by a White Paper issued under the authority of the Colonial Secretary, Lord Passfield. The report was bad enough; the White Paper was worse.[23]

Sir John found that apart from land held by Jews in reserve, there was in the short term 'and with the present methods of Arab cultivation' no land available for agricultural settlement by new immigrants. In the long term, he believed, a further 20,000 families could be admitted.

As for non-agricultural immigrants, he felt that where there were unemployed Arabs it was wrong 'that Jewish workmen from other countries should be imported to fill existing vacancies'. He added, however, that as Jewish capital was imported to employ Jewish labour, Arabs had nothing to gain from stopping either, and could have something to lose 'as the expenditure of that capital on wages will cause, ultimately, a demand for the services of a portion of the Arab unemployed'.

The White Paper omitted such reservations and accepted only Sir John's negative conclusions.

Dr Weizmann protested that the Paper was 'inconsistent with the terms of the Mandate, and in vital particulars marks the reversal of the policy hitherto followed by His Majesty's Government in regard to the Jewish National Home', and he and his leading associates on the broadened Jewish Agency, Felix Warburg and Lord Melchett, resigned.[24]

And the Jews were not alone to protest. A storm of criticism blew up inside the House of Commons and out, led by Lloyd George, Stanley Baldwin, Austen Chamberlain, Leopold Amery and Smuts.

On 14 February 1931, the Prime Minister, Ramsay MacDonald, in a letter to Dr Weizmann, published an interpretation of the White Paper which substantially altered its character.[25]

The 'landless Arabs', who under the White Paper as originally published would have had first claim on state lands hitherto earmarked for Jewish settlement, were now defined as 'such Arabs as can be shown to have been displaced from the lands which they occupied in consequence of the lands passing into Jewish hands, and who have not obtained other holdings . . . or other equally satisfactory occupation'. A 'prohibition of acquisition of additional land by Jews' was not implied, but merely 'such temporary controls . . . as may be necessary not to impair the harmony and effectiveness of the scheme of land settlement undertaken'. No stoppage of Jewish immigration was intended, nor did the government challenge the right of the Jewish Agency to employ only Jewish labour.

If the Jews had felt betrayed by the Passfield White Paper, the Arabs felt betrayed by MacDonald's interpretation. Whatever was recommended by Commissions of Inquiry, they felt, was always thwarted by the politicians in Westminster, and this latest and most dramatic reversal convinced them that there was nothing to be gained from negotiations. When riots next broke out they were directed largely against the British.

The Allies had shown slight recognition of Arab nationalism at the Peace Conference. They were aware of rumblings throughout the Middle East but took this to be part of the inevitable aftermath of war. Palestine in particular was a backward corner of a backward empire and it was felt that so long as the material conditions of its inhabitants were safeguarded there would be no strong opposition to the mass immigration of Jews. When opposition did arise it was naturally assumed that the Jewish agricultural policy tended to have an effect on the Arab peasantry akin to the Highland Clearances of the nineteenth century, and was creating a disgruntled class of land-less labourers. And that the agricultural settlements, by employing only Jews, were depriving Arabs not only of their land, but of a livelihood.

According to evidence given to the Shaw Commission, small areas, not exceeding 10 per cent of the land acquired by the Jews, were bought from peasants. The other areas had been acquired mostly from absentee owners of large estates.

In July 1931 the government appointed Lewis French, late of the Indian Civil Service, to head an Agricultural Development Com-mission, which had been recommended, among other measures, by Sir John Hope Simpson. Both Jews and Arabs refused to cooperate and the Commission never functioned, but French was able to look into the question of the 'discontented landless class' of Arabs, and found that it was neither so discontented, nor so landless, nor so large as was popularly imagined.

The Arabs, he found, sold land to the Jews, usually at good and occasionally at fantastic prices, and those who did so tended to fall into three main groups: the industrious peasant who sold part of his land, and improved the remainder with his profits; the non-industrious peasant who sold all his land and went on the debauch; and finally the landlord – usually absentee – who sold his land without thought for his tenants.[26]

A social problem did exist, but it was not entirely of the Jews' making.

The very pressure on Jews in eastern Europe to leave, the very numbers clamouring to get into Palestine, would in itself have imposed an obligation upon Jewish enterprises to favour Jewish labour. But there was also a philosophy involved. There was a determination that the Yishuv should be no mere transplantation of the ghetto. The Jewish society being created was a predominantly socialist one, imbued with Gordon's idea of the sanctity of labour. Some of the largest enterprises in the country, banks, insurance companies, civil engineers, were cooperative ones. And the kib-butzim and moshavim which were multiplying on Jewish National Fund land did not permit themselves to use even hired *Jewish* labour.

All this, of course, was no consolation to the Arabs. Nor was the fact that their standard of health, living, and their level of education was improving. The £78,000 spent on Arab education during 1921–2 increased five-fold within two decades. A well-educated class had come into being which found ready employment in government service. A later Commission which looked into the standards of social welfare reported:

> Though much more could have been done if more money had been available, the equipment of Palestine with social services is more advanced than any of its neighbours, and far more advanced than that of an Indian province or an African colony.[27]

But all that is no more relevant than the argument that a colonial administration was usually more efficient and less corrupt than an indigenous one. With all the benefits that the Jews were bringing, they also brought the threat of domination.

Some Jewish groups were aware of this and attempted to reach an understanding with the Arabs. Weizmann, as we have seen, had been able to persuade Feisal of the benefits which Arabs would receive from Jewish immigration, but he was unable to reconcile any influential Arab who came after him to the idea of a Jewish national home in Palestine. The Hashomer Hatzair, a political group on the extreme left, based largely on the kibbutz movement, sought an Arab-Jewish rapprochement through the principle of the unity of labour. And there was the Brit-Shalom, the Covenant of Peace, led by Dr Judah Magnes, President of the Hebrew University.

In 1942 Hashomer Hatzair joined with a group led by Chaim Kalvaryski, an aged veteran of the First Aliya, to form the League for Jewish-Arab Rapprochement and Cooperation, and plead for a bi-nationalist state.

In the same year Magnes extended his activities to form an Ichud, a union of all those anxious to secure Arab-Jewish cooperation, and attracted such influential Zionists as Henrietta Szold.

All these efforts proved abortive, for whatever support they might have found among the Jews, they received none from the Arabs.

After 1936 those moderate Arabs who might have been ready to cooperate with the Jews could have done so only at the risk of their lives. The Arabs of Palestine wanted what Arabs elsewhere were all beginning to acquire – their own independence, and that excluded any notion of a Jewish national home in their midst. Egypt, Iraq, Syria and Lebanon were, by the end of 1936, all enjoying almost complete sovereignty and Palestinian Arabs were anxious to join their ranks as a fully fledged state. And the longer they delayed the more the hope was threatened, for the influx of Jews was now enormous. Over 40,000 had entered Palestine in 1934, and over 60,000 in the following year – all as legal immigrants. And others were coming in overland through Syria (the French never lost an opportunity to embarrass Britain) or across the seas, illegally.

Arab faith in Britain was undermined by Ramsay MacDonald's letter to Weizmann. They felt that Jewish influence in the chancelleries of Europe was overwhelming, and if they were to keep Palestine Arab they could only depend on themselves. The fissiparous Arab political groups now began to form themselves into stable parties, and in 1935 they came together to demand democratic government, the prohibition of land sales to Jews, the immediate cessation of Jewish immigration, and an inquiry into the extent of illegal immigration.

The British administration, to the dismay of the Jewish Agency, went some distance towards meeting these demands. A democratic

48

body would have meant an Arab majority which in turn would have killed any hope of a Jewish national home.

The proposals aroused opposition in the House of Commons, and this confirmed the Arabs in their belief that they could not counter Jewish influence in London. If the idea of a Jewish national home was to be stifled they concluded it could only be stifled in Palestine.

In April 1936 the leaders of the various Arab parties constituted themselves into the Arab Higher Committee, under the Mufti. Local cells were formed. Violent outbreaks had already occurred earlier in the month. The AHC now declared a six-months general strike. Its extent and effectiveness showed that the opposition to the Mandate could not be dismissed as something instigated by political extremists or vested interests. It was a mass movement.

The strike was accompanied by violence. Civilians, troops and police were attacked, buildings were destroyed, crops set on fire, trains and motor convoys ambushed, bridges blown up, telegraph wires cut. Jews, who had hitherto exercised a policy of restraint, began to retaliate.

The High Commissioner promised a Royal Commission of Inquiry if the strike was called off. The Arabs replied that they had had their fill of commissions and inquiries. They demanded a cessation of immigration as a prior condition. Britain refused, but at the end of July 1936 a Royal Commission, under Lord Peel, was appointed. At the same time heavy reinforcements moved in from Egypt and Malta and the garrison was increased from 10,000 to 30,000 men. On 12 October the Arab strike was called off.

The Peel Commission found that the root cause of the 1936 disturbances was essentially that of all the disturbances which preceded it, 'namely the desire of the Arabs for national independence and their hatred and fear of the Jewish National Home'.[28]

There were in 1936, as there had been on the earlier occasions, numerous aggravating circumstances, but these did not affect the fundamental issue.

The Commission could offer no palliatives. It condemned the Mandate in its existing form as unworkable, and recommended partition. This, said the report, 'seems to offer at least a chance of ultimate peace. We can see none in any other plan.'

The increase in militancy among Arabs in the twenties and thirties was matched – possibly even provoked – by an increase in militancy among the Jews. Jabotinsky's Revisionists, who had come into being in 1925 with only 5 delegates at the Fourteenth Zionist Congress, grew rapidly. By 1931, with 52 delegates it was the third largest party in Congress. It had no doubt been given an impetus by both the 1929 riots and the Passfield White Paper, and there was a growing feeling, by no means limited to the Revisionists, that the policy of Weizmann had been too conciliatory. At the 1931 Congress, although he had already intimated that he needed a rest and would resign, a resolution of no confidence was passed against him. The Zionist movement was to regret this action, and four years later, after Jabotinsky and the Revisionists had broken away to form their own movement, he was recalled to the helm.[29]

Weizmann now entered upon what were perhaps the most challenging years of his career. The situation of the Jews in eastern Europe continued to be critical, that of German Jewry was desperate. He was convinced now, as he had been by the circumstances of 1922, that partition should not be rejected. Palestine, even in its truncated form, would provide an immediate and certain haven.

The Arabs rejected the scheme, and in June 1937 resumed their campaign of violence, attacking Jews, Britons and, with growing frequency, Arabs who had shown a readiness to cooperate with the administration or Jews.

The government, nevertheless, held on to the Peel plan and in April 1936 it sent out yet another Commission, under Sir John Woodhead, to see how it might be implemented. The Commission, however, found that the Peel partition scheme was unworkable. Instead it recommended an economic union between autonomous Jewish and Arab areas, with fiscal policy to be determined by Britain.[30]

The government, using the Woodhead Report as a basis for negotiations, now summoned a round table conference of Jewish and Arab leaders to consider future policy, including immigration, and indicated that in the absence of an agreed settlement within a stated period, it would impose its own.

If there had been a chance of an agreed Arab-Jewish settlement at any other time there was none when the London Conference convened in St James's Palace in March 1939.

The advent of Hitler in 1933, the Nuremberg laws in 1935, the Kristallnacht pogrom in 1938, the Austrian Anschluss, the rape of Czechoslovakia, the threat to Poland, had built up a vast movement of Jewish refugees. A Jewish state was no longer an ideological aspiration. It was becoming – to a degree which few could have anticipated – a matter of life and death.

The Arabs were aware of the pressure thus building up, which made them all the more determined to resist, and they were on strong ground. Another world war was imminent. Pan-Arab sentiments had been fired by the Palestine situation where the Arabs were now in more or less open revolt against the government, and the whole of Islam was becoming affected. A meeting of delegates representing all Arab states (except Yemen) at Bloudan near Damascus in September 1937, presided over by a former Prime Minister of Iraq, Tewfik es Suadi, demanded the annulment of the Balfour Declaration, and warned:

> We must make Great Britain understand that she must choose between our friendship and the Jews. Britain must change her policy in Palestine or we shall be at liberty to side with other European powers whose policies are inimical to Great Britain.[31]

Throughout 1938 Arab violence grew in intensity, with money and weapons pouring in from abroad, and by the end of the year there were nearly 2,000 dead – the great majority of them Arabs – and as many injured. Gradually the situation was brought under control, but over 20,000 British troops were involved in the military operation.

Britain could not afford to have such a force pinned down in war-time, nor could it afford a hostile Arab world.

The St James's Palace Conference proved wholly abortive. The Palestine Arabs refused to meet with the Jews, and a series of parallel

51

meetings had to be arranged. Neither side would listen to the case of the other, nor would either accept the proposals put forward by the government. On 17 March the Conference broke up. On the same day Germany invaded Czechoslovakia.

The government now published a White Paper containing its terms for a settlement.[32] As a policy it was entirely in keeping with the character of Munich. The Arabs had been the aggressors; the Jews were to be the victims. The Paper declared, *inter alia*, that only 75,000 Jews were to be admitted to Palestine during the next 5 years, including any who entered the country illegally. Further immigration at the end of that period would be subject to Arab consent. The Balfour Declaration was dead.

The White Paper did not satisfy the Arabs, it outraged the Jews, but as one historian put it: 'The government calculated quite correctly, that in the coming war the Jews would have no choice as to which side they supported . . . .'[33]

Ben Gurion, now Chairman of the Jewish Agency Executive, summed up the Zionist policy in the coming years: 'We shall fight in this war as if there was no White Paper, and we shall fight the White Paper as if there was no war.'[34]

4　　The end of the Mandate

AT THE OUTBREAK OF THE SECOND WORLD WAR
136,000 Jewish men and women in Palestine volunteered for service.
In the following year six battalions of troops, three Arab and three
Jewish, were raised and formed into the Palestine Regiment. Palestine
Jews also enlisted in the Pioneer Corps, the Army Service Corps,
the RAF and the Navy, as well as for special duties behind enemy
lines. By 1943 some 21,000 of them were involved in combatant
duties.

Zionist leaders were anxious that Jewish troops should be organized into a specifically Jewish fighting force, but commanders on
the spot, nervous of the possible political complications, opposed it.
In 1944, however, after the direct intervention of Winston Churchill,
a Jewish Brigade was formed. It fought with distinction on the
Italian front. It also, as hostilities came to an end, helped to form the
network for the movement of illegal immigrants to Palestine.

Under the treaty which gave her the Mandate over Palestine
Britain had been obliged to submit the 1939 White Paper to the
Permanent Mandates Commission of the League of Nations. The
PMC had found that its terms were not in accordance with those
of the Mandate. War broke out before the Council of the League
could comment, but the Jews had good grounds for viewing the
Paper as illegal. They certainly treated it as such.

Immigrants continued to come in, legally and illegally. Some
filtered their way through the Balkans and then overland through
Syria. Others came by sea. In the autumn of 1940 the navy stopped

a small flotilla of hulks, with some 3,000 immigrants on board, off the Palestine shore and transhipped them to other vessels for deportation. There were loud protests on ships and on shore, and one of the ships, the *Patria*, was holed by an explosion on board, and sank with the loss of 250 lives. A Commission of Inquiry found that the explosion was the work of a group on shore, aided by three or four people on board. (Later evidence suggests that the tragedy sprang from a clumsy attempt to disable the ship's engines and keep her in Haifa.)

In February 1942 the *Struma*, a cattle boat bound for Palestine with 769 men, women and children on board, but no papers, limped into Istanbul while frantic negotiations took place to get them immigration certificates. Before these could be completed the Turkish authorities ordered the ship to sea. On 24 February she blew up. There was only one survivor.

The *Struma* disaster, and the determination of the administration to enforce the provisions of the White Paper, caused a great deal of bitterness among Jews. It made it difficult for such moderates as Chaim Weizmann to maintain their influence in the Zionist movement. It led to the ascendancy of David Ben Gurion.

The Zionist Congress could not meet in the war years, but in May 1942 there took place in the Biltmore Hotel, New York, a conference of Jewish leaders on the future of Zionism, and there Ben Gurion carried through what came to be known as the Biltmore programme.

The programme, which went well beyond the stipulations of the Balfour Declaration, demanded that Palestine should be opened to unlimited immigration; that the Jewish Agency be vested with authority to control immigration and develop the country; that Palestine be established as a Jewish Commonwealth, and that a Jewish army be created.

The programme was adopted by the Zionist General Council, but opinion in the Jewish world was divided.

The programme was opposed by the New Immigration Party, which had been recently founded by German and Austrian Jews, who wanted to do nothing which might in any way hamper the

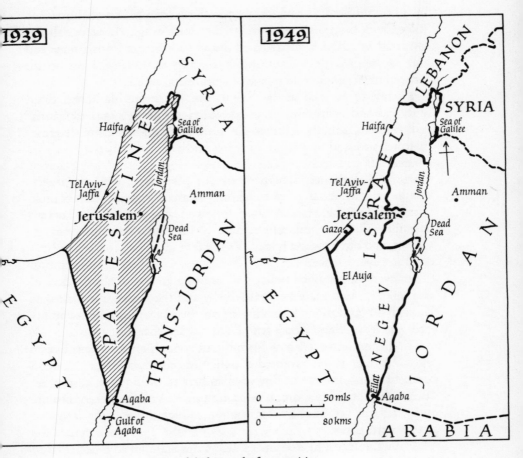

Israel before and after partition

war effort. They did not object to the ultimate aims of the programme, but they felt it was untimely. Others objected to the ultimate
aim. Hashomer Hatzair and Dr Magnes's Ichud still, at this late
date, hoped for some form of reconciliation with the Arabs in a
bi-national state.

During 1942 news began to seep through of the 'final solution'.
First reports were not believed, but they were too amply corroborated

by others. Hitler had embarked upon the extermination of European Jewry and from East and West the death-waggons were rolling towards Auschwitz. It hardened the attitude of the Jewish Agency, and as the government continued to apply the White Paper with full rigour, feelings were pushed to explosion point.

There had evolved in the Yishuv ever since the Hashomer days of the Second Aliya a voluntary defence force known as the Hagana which had gradually assumed the scale of a national army. It grew in secret and had to operate in secret and was based mainly on the cooperative settlements.

In the disturbances which shook the Mandate during the inter-war years individual Jews sometimes retaliated against Arab provocation, but the Hagana itself followed a policy of Havlaga – restraint. This became impossible as the outbreaks grew more violent, and one Hagana leader, Yitzchak Sadeh, developed a policy of aggressive defence.

But even the modified policy occasioned a great deal of impatience and in 1937, two years after Jabotinsky and the Revisionists left the Zionist Organization, his followers in the Hagana broke away to form the *Irgun Tzvai Leumi* (the National Defence Organization).

The Irgun, however, was not militant enough for all its elements, especially after it too assumed a policy of self-restraint on the outbreak of war, and even allowed members to volunteer for special duties with the British forces. A group under Abraham Stern broke away to form yet another organization, which came to be known as the Stern gang.

While the Irgun looked on Hitler as the main enemy, Stern saw the British Mandatory government in this role. Stern himself was killed by the police in February 1942, and twenty of his followers arrested, but the group continued to function till the end of the Mandate.

In January 1944, Irgun publicly called off its truce and went into action, under the command of Menachem Beigin. The Stern gang concentrated its efforts mainly against personnel, the Irgun against installations. In August the Stern gang made an attempt on the life of Sir Harold MacMichael, the retiring High Commissioner. On

6 November, they murdered Lord Moyne, Minister of State in Cairo.

This act horrified the Yishuv. The Jewish Agency gave the government the fullest cooperation, and the Hagana helped the police to hound down the terrorists. Within six months 279 members of the Stern gang and Irgun were arrested. The outrage seriously affected negotiations between Weizmann and the British government on a post-war settlement.

Winston Churchill had been among the most outspoken opponents of the 1939 White Paper, and had let Weizmann understand that Jews would be given full sovereignty in one sector of a partitioned Palestine with a Jerusalem enclave under British rule. Weizmann would have been disposed to accept it, but on this occasion he could not carry the Jewish Agency with him. The Vaad Leumi, the elected council of the Yishuv, also opposed partition. Both stood by the Biltmore programme.

In December 1944 at the annual conference of the British Labour Party, Mr Clement Attlee, on behalf of the National Executive, moved a resolution declaring:

> There is surely neither hope nor meaning in a 'Jewish National Home' unless we are prepared to let Jews, if they wish, enter this tiny land in such numbers as to become a majority. There was a strong case for this before the war. There is an inevitable case now, after the unspeakable atrocities of the cold and calculated German Nazi plan to kill all the Jews in Europe. Here, too, in Palestine surely is a case, on human grounds, and to promote a stable settlement, for transfer of population. Let the Arabs be encouraged to move out as the Jews move in.[35]

The latter part of this resolution, as Dr Weizmann observed, 'went beyond our own official policy'. Labour was more Zionist than the Zionists.

In July 1945 the Labour Party won an overwhelming victory at the polls. Four months later it formally repudiated the 1944 resolution, and offered instead yet another Commission of Inquiry.

President Truman had a little earlier pressed the British government to admit 100,000 Jews into Palestine at once. The holocaust

which had overtaken European Jewry strengthened Zionist sentiment everywhere and especially among the Jews of America who
now formed the mass following of the Zionist movement.

In 1944 resolutions were tabled in the US Senate and House of
Representatives which would have virtually committed Congress
to the Biltmore programme, but the War Department was alarmed
at the repercussions they could have on the Arabs and the resolutions
were not passed.[36] Later the same year, however, in his last Presi-
dential election, President Roosevelt promised American Zionists
that if re-elected he would help to bring about 'the establishment of
Palestine as a free and democratic Jewish commonwealth'.

He was re-elected but it fell to President Truman to redeem the
promise. His request to Britain to let 100,000 Jews into Palestine
was as far as he could go. America was acquiring important
interests in Saudi Arabia and Roosevelt had promised King Ibn
Sa'ud that he would do nothing 'which might prove hostile to the
Arab people'.

President Truman's intervention was not kindly received in
London, but America's growing interest in the Middle East enabled
the government to widen the basis of the forthcoming inquiry. An
Anglo-American Commission, consisting of six members from
each country, was announced on 13 November. It was required,
among other things, 'to examine political, economic, and social conditions in Palestine as they bear upon the problem of Jewish
immigration . . . to examine the position of the Jews in those
countries in Europe where they have been the victims of Nazi and
Fascist persecution'. In the meantime terrorist incidents multiplied
and it was becoming evident that they were not entirely the work of
Irgun or the Stern gang. Weizmann, always a moderating influence,
was a revered figure in the Yishuv, to which he returned in 1944
after an absence of five years, but he was already looked on as
belonging to a bygone age. He continued to be President of the
Zionist Organization, but the effective man at the head of affairs
was Ben Gurion.

Ben Gurion had lost faith in the great powers, their performance
inevitably fell short of their promises, and he gradually became

a *Sinn Feiner*. He could not see a Jewish state emerging without a war with the Arabs, and in such a situation Jews would be able to rely only on themselves. Addressing a Jewish youth rally at Tel-Hai on 20 March 1943, he warned them to prepare for the battle which would come at the end of the war.

Strenuous efforts were made to secure arms from every available source and in August, September and December of 1944 there took place a dramatic series of trials of Jews and British deserters, for the theft of arms and explosives from British military installations.

In 1945, after the war in Germany was over, Ben Gurion anticipated that a substantial part of America's vast armament industry was about to be dismantled and he sent Chaim Slavin, head of the Hagana's secret arms industry, and Ya'akov Dori, head of the Hagana, to acquire some of the machinery, which was at once shipped to Palestine.

On 31 October, while Weizmann and Ben Gurion were engaged in negotiations with the government in London, the Haifa oil refinery was attacked, the railway station at Lydda blown up, three small naval craft were sunk, and railway lines cut at fifty different points. It was all performed with perfect efficiency and little loss of life. It had been a combined operation between the *Palmach*, spearhead of the Hagana, the Irgun and the Stern gang.

Illegal immigration continued.

The Anglo-American Commission began its work at the end of 1945 with the assurance from the British Foreign Secretary Ernest Bevin that if it returned a unanimous report he would do everything in his power to implement it.[37]

The report, which appeared in April 1946, was unanimous, but was rejected. It urged that 100,000 Jews should be allowed into Palestine at once and that the government should facilitate further Jewish immigration under suitable conditions. It also recommended that the restrictions on Jewish land purchase should be ended, but that at the same time the exclusion of Arab labour from Jewish National Fund enterprises should be made illegal. It believed that Palestine should be a bi-national state governed under a system of trusteeship.

On 1 May Mr Attlee told the House of Commons that there was no question of 100,000 Jews being admitted until the 'illegal' armies in Palestine, Jewish and Arab, laid down their arms.

On 12 June Mr Bevin told the Labour Party Conference that to let a further 100,000 Jews into Palestine would need another division of troops and would cost the country £200,000,000. A few days later nine bridges, including the Allenby bridge over the Jordan, were demolished. Kol Yisrael, the 'Voice of Israel', the secret radio of the Hagana, accepted full responsibility for the raid on behalf of the 'resistance movement'. The Yishuv was in almost open revolt.

The government replied on 29 June by occupying the Jewish Agency building and arresting a number of Jewish leaders, including Moshe Shertok, Rabbi Fishman, David Remez and Dov Joseph. (Ben Gurion was in Paris and remained there until the hue and cry was over.) At the same time many leading members of the Palmach were taken into custody, and a large arms cache was discovered at Kibbutz Yagur, a Palmach stronghold.

Three weeks later a wing of the King David Hotel, Jerusalem, part of which was used as British Army Headquarters, was blown up with the loss of 91 lives, British, Jewish and Arab. The Irgun was responsible, though Menachem Beigin claims that the Hagana was also implicated.

In the meantime there was much coming and going between London and Washington in an attempt to devise a settlement, and at the end of July a committee of Anglo-American experts came out with yet another partition scheme. It would have allowed Jews and Arabs their own autonomous regions, with control of their own affairs, including immigration – though within the limits of their absorptive capacity. The proposed Jewish area was smaller than in the 1937 Peel partition plan, and the degree of autonomy fell short of full independence. The fact that 100,000 Jews would have been admitted to Palestine within a year of the acceptance of the plan did not outweigh the objections to it.[38]

The Jewish Agency made counter-proposals which would have given the Jewish state frontiers not unlike those of Israel today, with

Jerusalem as part of an international zone. This was a considerable retreat on the Biltmore programme and it was as far as the Agency was willing to go.

The Arabs had also rejected the autonomy proposals, and a conference which the British government had called in London, to consider them, was adjourned pending further discussion.

At the Twenty-Second Zionist Congress, the first since the war, Weizmann appealed for an understanding with Britain on a Jewish state in an 'adequate' part of Palestine. Congress, which now had a large American contingent, was in no mood to do so. It rejected his appeal by 171 votes to 154, and resolved to boycott the London Conference once it was resumed.[39]

Jewish leaders did, however, attend parallel talks with the Colonial Secretary, Mr Creech Jones, while the Conference was being held, but there was never for a moment any hope of a settlement even remotely acceptable to both sides, and the government, in despair, referred the whole issue to the United Nations.

The stumbling block had, of course, been the question of immigration. To the Jews, apart from the acute need of finding a home for tens of thousands of their fellows still rotting in displaced persons' camps, there was the fear that independence for Palestine while they still formed only a third of the population would limit them to permanent minority status.

And even if, as now seemed probable, some partition scheme should emerge, the boundary lines would rest largely on population densities and areas of settlement. Every ship-load of immigrants smuggled in could mean so many more acres of Palestine under the Jewish flag. It was an issue on which neither Jews nor Arabs felt able to make concessions.

The movement of illegal immigrants, as we have seen, had already begun, albeit on a very minor scale, in 1927, and continued throughout the thirties and the war. It was accelerated immediately after the cessation of hostilities when, with the aid of the Jewish Brigade and Jewish personnel working in the refugee camps, an extensive network was formed for the movement of Jews across Europe to assembly points on the Mediterranean.

The quota of 75,000 Jewish immigrants permitted under the 1939 White Paper was exhausted by 1945, but the government continued to admit a further 1,500 immigrants a month pending a Palestine settlement. The number of Jews arriving far exceeded that total, and special detention camps were set up in Cyprus. But the ships continued to come. A few managed to elude the authorities, most were intercepted, and their transhipment often resulted in hostile demonstrations. On 13 August, after 600 immigrants from the 200-ton vessel *Henrietta Szold* had been forcibly transhipped, there were riots in Haifa resulting in the death of 3 Jews and the injury of 10 others. There was a protest strike in Jerusalem, and the Vaad Leumi announced a policy of non-cooperation.

And still the ships came, large and small: the *Smyrna*, 760 tons, carrying 1,662 immigrants; the *Palmach*, 300 tons with 626 immigrants; the *San Dimitrio*, 733 tons, with 1,279; the *Hagana*, 1,039 tons and 2,678.

On 18 July the biggest vessel involved in the traffic, the *Exodus*, of 1,814 tons and with 4,550 men, women and children on board, was brought into Haifa harbour after a three-hour struggle with a naval boarding party in which the ship's mate was killed, and three members of the boarding party were injured. The passengers, survivors of Nazi death camps who had been living in displaced persons' camps in Germany, were now, to the dismay of the Jewish world, returned to Germany.

In November 1946 Mr Shertok and the other Jewish Agency leaders who had been arrested the previous June were released from detention, and there followed a few weeks of comparative calm. Then on 1 January 1947, the clandestine Irgun radio announced the intensification of attacks against British troops. The occasion was a sentence of death passed on one of their members, Dov Gruner, for his part in an attack on a police station. A few weeks later Mr H. I. Collins, a retired army major, and Judge Ralph Windham, President of the Tel-Aviv District Court, were kidnapped at the point of a gun. On 27 January the High Commissioner, Sir Alan Cunningham, summoned Golda Meir (head of the Political Department of the Jewish Agency), Mr Eliezer Kaplan (the

Treasurer) and Mr Israel Rokach (Mayor of Tel-Aviv) and warned them that unless Judge Windham and Mr Collins were released on the following day, he would impose martial law. At the same time the execution of Gruner was stayed. Judge Windham was found unharmed the following day, and Mr Collins on 30 January. On 16 April Gruner was hanged.

The Palestine issue came before the United Nations in April 1947 and it decided to set up a Special Commission on Palestine to consist of eleven neutral states, Australia, Canada, Czechoslovakia, Guatemala, India, Iran, the Netherlands, Peru, Sweden, Uruguay and Yugoslavia.

The United Nations Special Commission on Palestine, UNSCOP, as it came to be known, was in Palestine in July and was able to witness the sick being disembarked from the *Exodus* and the rest of the immigrants transhipped to three British vessels to be returned to their port of origin.

On 1 September UNSCOP published its report and recommended yet another partition scheme. It allotted the Jews a more generous area than any previous scheme, including the Valley of Jezreel, eastern Galilee, much of the coastal plain, and the Negev. Jerusalem and an enclave round it would be under international trusteeship. The Indian, Iranian and Yugoslav members of the Commission dissented and issued a minority report more favourable to the Arabs.

The Arab League, which had been brought together by Britain in 1945 to further Arab unity, was united at least on the Palestine question, and it rejected both the majority and minority reports.

In May 1946 the Mufti, who had been kept in rather easy circumstances as a prisoner in France, escaped and arrived in Cairo. Within a few months he was back at the helm of Palestine Arab affairs from which he had been dislodged by Britain in 1937. The Council of the Arab League made over to him all funds which it had amassed for Palestine purposes, and he resumed control of the Arab Higher Committee. He now warned that any attempt to impose partition would mean war. 'We Arabs shall not be the losers,' he said. 'We shall be fighting on our own ground and shall be supported not only by 70,000,000 Arabs around us but by 400,000,000 Moslems.'[40]

The Zionist General Council, meeting in Zurich on 3 September, approved the majority report by 61 votes to 6.

The United Nations formed a special *ad hoc* committee on Palestine, and the debate on the UNSCOP report opened under threatening clouds.

Britain made it clear that she did not accept the Commission's scheme, nor would she impose it on either Arabs or Jews against their will, and that in the absence of a settlement she would withdraw from Palestine.

In the debate which followed, the Jewish area was whittled down by some 500 square miles, but this too was accepted by the Jews. The proposals were recommended to the United Nations by both America and the Soviet Union, and on 29 November they were passed, and Tel-Aviv went delirious.

It is unnecessary to consider the UN proposals in detail here. The borders of the Jewish state were to be determined not in the council chambers but on the battlefield.

The Palestine Arab Higher Committee met in Jerusalem on 30 November, rejected the partition scheme outright, and ordered a general strike of Arabs throughout Palestine. The strike was accompanied by widespread violence and on 7 December the Jewish Agency ordered all Jews aged 17–25 to register for 'security and other essential services'.

Arab attack was followed by Jewish counter-attack, and incidents grew in number and gravity. On Christmas Day over 100 Jews and Arabs were killed in different parts of the country.

On 30 December, after 6 Haifa Arabs had been killed by a bomb thrown from a passing vehicle, there was a massacre of Jewish workers in the refinery. By the time troops arrived to restore order, 41 were killed and 15 injured.

In the new year large Arab bands calling themselves 'the Palestine Army of Liberation' came over the Syrian border and attacked Jewish settlements in the north. They were led by Fawzi al-Kawakji, a veteran of countless campaigns who had been active against the Mandatory government a decade earlier, but he was held in check without great difficulty.

The main cause of concern was Jerusalem. It was isolated from the principal areas of Jewish settlement and depended upon a regular flow of provisions from Tel-Aviv through Arab-held hill country. All supplies had to be organized in convoys and their passage was an extremely perilous undertaking.[41] The siege, which began in December 1947, was eased a little when the Hagana took Castel, which dominates the main approach to the city, in April. Inside the city, there was heavy fighting with serious loss of life.

On 9 April, while the struggle for Castel was at its height, the near-by village of Deir Yassin was taken by the Irgun and the Stern gang after heavy fighting, and most of its inhabitants, 254 men, women and children, were massacred.

The details, broadcast over the Arab networks, alarmed the Arab population. There had been a movement of more prosperous Arabs out of the country as soon as the fighting began. News of Deir Yassin quickened the flow to an exodus. On 18 April the 6,000 Arabs of Tiberias fled from the town. On 22 April fighting broke out for the control of Haifa. By the end of the day it was effectively in Jewish hands. The Mayor of the city, Mr Shabtai Levy, had tried to persuade the local Arabs to remain, but they were urged by their leaders to move northwards over the border, and by the end of the following day some 40,000 of them had fled.

In this early stage of the fighting the Jews were critically short of arms. The Hagana was still illegal and even while Britain was preparing for withdrawal arms searches continued and caches were confiscated.

At the outbreak of hostilities the Jews had some 15,000 weapons in all, including rifles, light machine-guns, and a few 3-inch mortars. The Hagana also had its own arsenal manufacturing explosives and sub-machine guns, but the Jews nevertheless had fewer arms than men to bear them.

In November, Ben Gurion dispatched Ehud Avriel on a purchasing mission to Europe and he returned with a large quantity of arms from Czechoslovakia, including 10,000 rifles and 450 machine guns. By the middle of April the Jews, who had been hard-pressed all winter, were able to go over to the offensive.

Britain had announced that she would abandon the Mandate on 15 May and the Jewish Agency together with the Vaad Leumi had completed plans for a provisional Jewish state, when President Truman suggested that as an emergency measure the Mandate should be succeeded by a 'temporary UN trusteeship for Palestine to provide a government and keep the peace'. The plan was welcomed by the Arab League, but emphatically rejected by the Jews. In the meantime the fighting continued. The Hagana dislodged Fawzi al-Kawakji's 'Palestine Liberation Army' from Safad, and on 28 April, in a joint action with the Irgun, it launched an attack on Jaffa, a wholly Arab town which under the partition scheme had been allocated to the Arabs. A cease-fire was arranged after British intervention, but much of the town was devastated and most of its inhabitants had fled. On 12 May it surrendered to the Jews.

Fighting in the Old City of Jerusalem was brought to a halt by the intervention of the Trusteeship Council of the United Nations on 2 May. On the initiative of the High Commissioner the truce was extended to the new city on 7 May, and was substantially observed by both sides until the termination of the Mandate.

At 9 a.m. on 14 May, the last British High Commissioner slipped out of Haifa almost unnoticed. The Union Jacks were hauled down. Twenty-five years of British rule were at an end. They had begun with extravagant hopes.

In 1917 the Near and Middle East was still thought of as at the disposal of Europe to be carved up and allocated among the powers according to their spheres of interest: Iraq and Palestine to Britain; Syria to the French; a slice of Turkey to the Greeks. The belief was shattered by Ataturk when he threw the Greeks into the Mediterranean, and the inhabitants of Turkey's former Arab possessions also began to assert themselves.

When Britain promised a Jewish home in Palestine in November 1917 the possibility of her doing so was already then hardly within her power, and it receded with every passing year. When Churchill carved out a kingdom for Abdullah in Transjordan in 1922 he might still have been able to impose a Jewish state upon the Arabs of Palestine, but the Jews were not yet there in sufficient numbers.

There were 83,000 of them and they formed only 11 per cent of the population. They were too few even for a Jewish state *within* Palestine. By 1936, when their numbers had grown to 400,000 and they formed almost a third of the population, they were too scattered. The Peel partition plan would have left 250,000 Arabs in the Jewish areas of Palestine, and 150,000 Jews in the Arab areas. Palestine, moreover, could not be insulated from political developments in Egypt, Syria and Iraq. Arab nationalism had grown in virulence and at the height of the 1936–8 rebellion some 30,000 British troops were tied down in Palestine, and this while the war clouds were gathering in Europe.

Partition could have been imposed only at immense expense and with a large army, and once in being there was every likelihood that large forces would still be tied up in keeping the peace. An area so near to what was thought of as 'the life-line of the Empire' could not be left in chaos. On the other hand the plight of German Jewry, and the threat to Czech and Polish Jews posed by the ambitions of Hitler – to forget, for the time being, the Balfour Declaration – imposed a moral obligation on Britain to keep Palestine open.

But it was an age in which moral obligations were not taken very seriously.

Giving evidence before the Peel Commission Weizmann said that there were in eastern Europe 'six million people doomed to be pent up in a place where they are not wanted, and for whom the world is divided into places where they cannot live, and places where they cannot enter'.

This was no mere rhetoric.

A conference on refugees at Evian in July 1938 heard a great many humane sentiments, but it resulted in little practical action. Of all the nations present, Dominica alone agreed to throw her doors open to Jews from Germany and Austria without delay.

(America later undertook to admit 30,000 Jews a year from Germany. Britain eventually admitted 100,000 Jews between 1938 and 1940, and Australia 15,000. South Africa let in only those with close relatives in the Union.)

The war offered Britain a way out, and she took it at the expense of the Jews. It is difficult to believe that a nation which could have made so far-seeing and imaginative a gesture as the Balfour Declaration could have been guilty of such a retreat, but it is unlikely that any nation in Britain's position in 1939 would have done anything else. It was difficult for even the most moderate Jews to appreciate this. The great redeemer had become the great betrayer. Thereafter the rise of Ben Gurion and Jewish Sinn Feinism was inevitable.

The sorriest chapter in the history of the Mandate is, however, the post-war one.

European Jewry had been virtually extirpated and the few Jews who remained had no wish to end their days amid the ashes of their former homes. The Arab share in the allied war effort had been meagre where it was not obstructive. While Britain still thought in terms of Imperial or Commonwealth communications, a Jewish state in Palestine as a member of the Commonwealth would have been not only an historic act of humanity and restitution, but it would have given her the secure base she needed.

And even if, as she finally concluded, the creation of a Jewish state under her aegis would have cost her too much in men and money, she might have withdrawn from her role with a certain grace. But instead, she continued to hound the Hagana, without which no Jew in Palestine could have passed a night in safety, and she continued almost to the last minute to search for Jewish arms and to impound them. And when in December 1947 the Arabs began the war against the Jews she did little to check them, or to impede the movement of Kawakji's bands over the Syrian frontier. Nor did she do anything to help the UN or assist to implement UN proposals once she had washed her hands of the Mandate.

Britain had passed through a trying period. 'But when all allowance is made for frayed nerves and the weariness of long service in years of strain', concluded Christopher Sykes in Cross Roads to

Israel, his superb study of the emergence of the Jewish state, 'it does seem that after November 1947 an element of embittered cussedness, and the madness that goes with it, became a part of British policy.'

On 15 May 1948 was the Jewish Sabbath. At 4 p.m. on the 14th a specially convened body calling itself the National Council and made up of representatives of the Zionist Executive, the Vaad Leumi and parties who belonged to neither, met in the Tel-Aviv Museum of Modern Art, and there, under the chairmanship of David Ben Gurion, the State of Israel was proclaimed.

> The state will be open to all immigrants, will promote the development of the country for all its inhabitants, will be based on the precepts of liberty, justice and peace taught by the Hebrew prophets, will uphold full social and political equality for all its citizens without distinction of race, creed or sex and will guarantee full freedom of education and culture.

The state undertook to abide by the principles of the United Nations Charter, promised to safeguard the shrines and holy places of all religions, assured equality of citizenship to all Arab inhabitants.

It was an historic occasion, but not one for immediate rejoicing. The day before, the Etzion bloc, a group of four religious kibbutzim in the Hebron area to the south of Jerusalem, fell after heavy fighting, and the Arab grip on the Old City tightened. On 16 May 1948 the Arabs penetrated the Jewish quarter. Hope rose two days later when the Palmach took Mount Zion adjacent to the Old City, but on the same day local Arab troops were reinforced by the Legion. On 28 May old Jerusalem fell.[42]

The capture of Castel had cleared the immediate approaches to the new part of Jerusalem, but farther west the supply route was still dominated by the Arab-held police post at Latrun, and a new road was cut through the hills to by-pass it.

In the south the Egyptians made a rapid advance, with one fork reaching to within twenty miles of Tel-Aviv, and another within sight of Jerusalem, but they were checked at both points and from there forced to retreat. In the north the Hagana took Acre and the Syrian army was kept in check. In the centre the Iraqi army, though defeated near Beisan in the Jordan valley, thrust westward to within ten miles of the sea.

On 20 May the United Nations had appointed a mediator, Count Folke Bernadotte, President of the Swedish Red Cross, and on 11 June he arranged a truce to run for four weeks. It was during this period, and while still hemmed in by Arab armies on all sides, that the Jews suddenly found themselves faced with the prospect of civil war.

Ben Gurion had always been concerned to keep all Jewish forces under unified command. The crack units of Palmach were, against the wishes of their commanders, fully integrated into the Hagana and on 26 May the latter had been formally reconstituted into the Israel Defence Forces, and a decree had been issued forbidding anyone to hold arms in any force outside the IDF. The Hagana had, after 1945, from time to time carried out combined operations with both the Stern gang and Irgun. The Sternists were disbanded after the Declaration of Independence, and on 1 June Irgun undertook to enrol its members into the IDF. The undertaking was not wholly observed.

On 18 June 1948, during the first truce, a ship appeared off the northern shore of Israel with a cargo of arms for the Irgun. When ordered to surrender the cargo the ship refused and made south for Tel-Aviv, where it was beached. There the authorities repeated the order and when it was again ignored the ship was sunk after several direct hits from army mortars.

Trouble spread to the shore and there were clashes in the streets of Tel-Aviv between Irgun supporters and the army. Fifteen people were killed and many others injured before the situation was brought under control.

On 23 June Tel-Aviv was placed under curfew and some 400 members of the Irgun were arrested.

The danger of civil war was averted, but that did not end the trouble with extremists. On 17 September Count Bernadotte, who had been trying in vain to reach a compromise settlement between Jews and Arabs, was assassinated by former members of the Stern gang.

The government at once imposed a curfew on Jerusalem and rounded up some 200 former Sternists and their sympathizers. At the same time the Irgun was presented with a final ultimatum to surrender its arms and enlist in the IDF, or be faced with military action. The government on this occasion looked as if it meant business, and Irgun complied.

Attempts which were made to extend the first truce failed through the intransigence of Egypt and Syria and on 6 July fighting was resumed. In the ten days which followed before the next cease-fire, Israel took Nazareth, Ramleh, Lydda and Lydda airport. The gains in this last sector opened the corridor to Jerusalem.

The second truce lasted for nearly three months but after numerous breaches of the agreement by the Egyptians on the southern front, the Israeli forces resumed action on 15 October.

On 21 October they took Beersheba.

In the north Kawakji's 'Palestine Liberation Army' was chased in disorder over the Lebanese border and Galilee was cleared.

The Jews were helped by divisions among the Arabs. A month earlier on 22 September the Palestine Arab Higher Committee had announced the formation of a 'Palestine government' based in Gaza, and claiming authority over the whole of Palestine. King Abdullah countered by having himself proclaimed king of Arab Palestine at a hand-picked meeting of notables on 1 October. At about the same time a local truce on the Jerusalem front was negotiated between Jews and the Arab Legion.

On 23 December Israel launched a combined land, sea and air attack on the Egyptians, inflicting heavy losses in men and equipment, and forcing a further withdrawal. When the fighting was brought to a halt by the intervention of the UN Security Council on 7 January 1949, the Egyptians were left with only a small strip round Gaza.

Pressure had been building up from the Security Council on both Jews and Arabs to call a halt to the fighting. Dr Ralph Bunche, who had replaced Count Bernadotte as UN mediator, finally brought Egypt and Israel together on the island of Rhodes, and on 24 February they signed an armistice agreement which defined Israel's southern frontier. Similar agreements were signed with Lebanon on 23 March, Jordan on 3 April and Syria on 29 July. There was no armistice with Iraq, who had withdrawn her forces from Palestine and who had no contiguous frontier with it.

In December 1948 the Security Council established a Conciliation Commission to negotiate permanent peace treaties between Israel and her neighbours, but its efforts have proved fruitless, and Israel's frontiers, until 5 June 1967, were those laid down in the various armistice agreements.

Jerusalem, which under the UN plan was to have been part of an international zone, was divided between Israel and Jordan. In December 1949 the United Nations again called for the internationalization of Jerusalem, but the resolution was rejected by both Israel and Jordan. In 1950 Jerusalem was proclaimed the capital of Israel.

5   The sinews of statehood

THE JEWISH STATE HAD NOT BEEN BORN out of chaos.

By the end of the Mandate, in spite of the inter-communal strife, there was already in existence a well tried system of local government which had been established by Sir Arthur Wauchope, the British High Commissioner, in 1934. There was a judicial system. There was the Vaad Leumi. There was an educational system. There were institutions of higher learning. There was the Hagana. There was, what was almost a state within a state, the Histadrut.

The Histadrut was founded in 1920 by Ben Gurion and a number of associates in the Jewish labour movement, and rapidly made its mark on the Yishuv. It began with 4,433 members. Today it has nearly a million, both Jew and Arab. It exists to protect the right of the worker, but it is far more than a trade union, and also includes self-employed and professional men.

The supreme body of the Histadrut is the *Veida*, the General Assembly, whose members are elected by proportional representation. These elections are hotly contested on party lines, and since the formation of Mapai in 1930 it has, like the Zionist Organization and the Vaad Leumi, been dominated by that party.

The Veida elects the *Moatza*, the General Council, which directs Histadrut policy between sessions of the Assembly. The Council elects the *Vaad Hapoel*, the Executive Committee, and finally, at the very head of the pyramid, stands the Secretariat which is elected by the Executive Committee.

The Histadrut controls numerous mutual-aid institutions like the Kupat Holim, the Workers' Sick Fund, which looks after the health of 70·3 per cent of the population, and runs 14 hospitals with 2,981 beds, 14 convalescent homes and over 1,000 clinics. The Kupat Holim, in fact, is a virtual national health service.

The Histadrut publishes *Davar*, one of the largest and most influential daily papers in the country, and owns the Am Oved publishing house. The Ohel Theatre was run under its aegis, and the Hapoel Sports Association. It also maintains libraries, organizes extramural courses, lectures and concerts for workers, and has a travelling film library which serves agricultural settlements and out/lying villages. It runs a Working Men's College. It has an Arab section to help Arab workers and peasants in cooperative production and marketing. It is the biggest employer in the country and the output of its various affiliated enterprises is responsible for about a quarter of the gross national product.

These enterprises are controlled by the Hevrat Ovdim, the General Cooperative Association of Jewish Workers, and include: Almost all the kibbutzim and moshavim (collective and co/operative settlements). Tnuva (The Central Agricultural Marketing Cooperative), which markets some 70 per cent of the country's agricultural output and maintains a chain of popular restaurants; its turnover in 1964 was worth about IL454,000,000. Hamashbir Hamerkazi (The Central Wholesale Supply Cooperative) which acts as supplier for kibbutzim, moshavim and local consumers' cooperatives; H.H. in turn owns wholly or in part numerous industrial enterprises, including the Shemen Oil and Soap Works; Hamashbir Flour Mills; Hatzamar Wool Processing; Fertilizers and Chemicals Ltd.; Minaal Shoe Factory; Hamegaper Rubber Products. It is the largest trading organization in Israel; its turnover in 1964 totalled IL330,000,000. Solel Bone, the largest contractor in Israel, which owns among other things, numerous enterprises connected with building, including the Nesher Cement Works; Vulcan Foundries; Phoenicia Glass Works; Lime and Stone Production Company; and the Kharsa Ceramic Works, all of them grouped in a holding company with a turnover of about IL360,000,000 and over 9,000 employees. Solel Bone alone has some 30,000 employees and an annual turnover of about IL460,000,000.

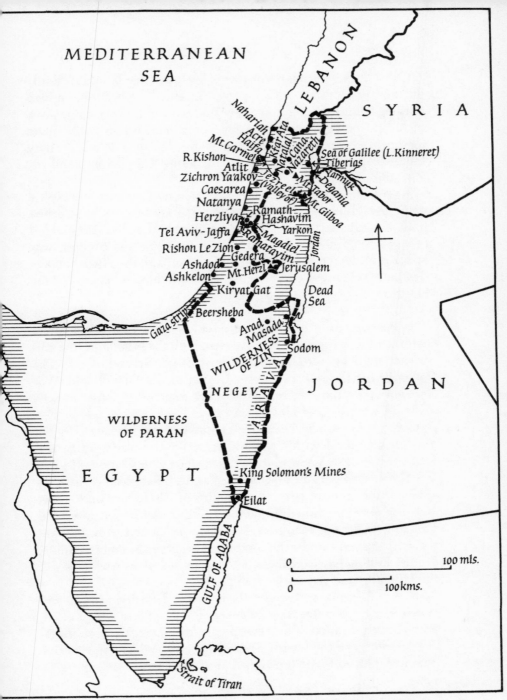

MEDITERRANEAN
SEA

LEBANON

SYRIA

Nahariah
Acre
Haifa
Mt.Carmel
Kfar Ata
Mtalah
Cana
Nazareth
Sea of Galilee (L.Kinneret)
Tiberias
R. Kishon
Atlit
Zichron Ya'akov
Caesarea
Natanya
Herzliya
Tel Aviv-Jaffa
Rishon Le Zion
Ashdod
Ashkelon
Mt.Herzl
Kiryat Gat
Beersheba
Gaza Strip

e-Jezreel
(Valley of)
Mt.Tabor
Mt.Gilboa
Degania
Yarmuk

Ramath
Hashavim
Yarkon
Ramatayim
Magdiel
Jordan
Gedera
Jerusalem

Dead
Sea

Arad
Masada
Sodom

WILDERNESS
OF ZIN

NEGEV

ARAVA

JORDAN

WILDERNESS
OF PARAN

EGYPT

King Solomon's Mines

Eilat

GULF OF AQABA

Strait of Tiran

0   100 mls.

0   100 kms.

*Political map of Israel. (The shaded area indicates territory captured from the Arabs
in the 1967 war)*

Other Hevrat Ovdim enterprises include: the Workers' Bank, the Hassne Insurance Company, Shikun Limited (a workers' housing company), and some 200 producers and service companies, including the Egged and Dan bus companies. It also holds shares in the Nachson Fishing Company, the Mekorot Water Supply Company, the American Palestine Trading Corporation, and the Zim shipping line.

As the Histadrut grew it created a large, well-trained and highly professional bureaucracy, whose services, if need be, could be called upon for external duties. Thus the Mossad La'aliya Bet, which brought 105,000 Jewish illegal immigrants into the country, was operated under the auspices of the Histadrut, and the Histadrut was also intimately involved in the gradual evolution and control of the Hagana.

The Hagana, as is often the case with such organizations, grew haphazardly. It began, as we have seen, with the Hashomer, the self-defence units founded by the pioneers of the Second Aliya. The Palestine battalion of the Jewish Legion in the First World War provided prospective recruits, including some of its future leaders, Eliahu Golomb, Dov Hos and Ya'akov Dori.

Golomb in particular was the architect of the Hagana. He had tried to keep the Jewish Legion intact at the end of hostilities, and when this became impossible he urged upon Ben Gurion and Ben Zvi the need to train an underground army. That need became very evident in the riots of 1921. The number of self-defence units grew, but they were individualistic, loosely linked and under no central guidance. After the 1929 riots, however, the Vaad Leumi brought the various groups under the control of a security committee of nine, headed by Pinchas Rutenberg, and composed of representatives of the Histadrut and right-wing groups.

In 1936, during the Arab rebellion, the British recruited and armed some 3,000 Jewish Settlement Police. Then and, indeed, until the very creation of the Jewish state, the Hagana was an illegal organization, and the Jewish Settlement Police, which largely came from its ranks, virtually functioned as its legal arm.

During the Arab rebellion the Hagana became restive under the policy of restraint imposed by the Jewish Agency, and gradually, as the rebellion grew, some of its units moved out of their purely defensive role and went over to the offensive.

Major Orde Wingate, in 1938 an intelligence officer with the British army in Palestine, and a passionate believer in Zionism, incorporated a number of these units into Special Night Squads which he trained at Kibbutz Ein Harod in the Valley of Jezreel.

During the war the Hagana, while still illegal, began to train commando units for operations under British command behind the enemy lines. This was the beginning of the Palmach. One such unit, consisting of 23 men, was sent in May 1941 to blow up oil-installations in Vichy-held Tripoli. It failed disastrously and all the men were wiped out.

In the following month, as British troops moved into Syria, Hagana volunteers went ahead to disrupt communications and act as guides. Among them were Yigal Allon, who commanded the southern front during the War of Liberation, and Moshe Dayan (later the victor of Sinai) who lost an eye in the operation.

In September 1944 the Jewish Brigade was established and it proved a natural recruiting ground for the Hagana. By the time the war was over, the Jews had a firm nucleus of seasoned men, trained in the intricacies of modern war. There were some 2,500 men in the Palmach itself.

The work of the Hagana was from its earliest days bedevilled by political factionalism and right up to 1948 it was controlled by a coalition consisting of nominees from the Histadrut, which is to say Mapai and its left-wing associates, and a number of right-wing groups who in turn, theoretically at least, were answerable to the Vaad Leumi and the Jewish Agency. It was not until September 1949 that the Israeli forces were formally constituted by the Defence Services Law, and command vested with the Minister of Defence.

In 1950 the Noar Halutzi Lohem, the Fighting Pioneer Youth, known as Nahal, which gives young conscripts an agricultural as well as a military training, was established. In its first two years Nahal set up fifteen agricultural settlements in strategic border areas.

There is also the Gadna cadet force for young people aged 14–18 which is under the joint control of the Ministry of Education and Defence and in which a military training is again combined with training in agriculture.[43]

Although the Hagana began as a purely volunteer force, Israel has never been able to dispense with conscription. The length of National Service has tended to vary with the frontier situation. Men and women are both liable to conscription, though the latter may claim exemption on religious grounds. Men remain on the reserve list till they are 49 and women till they are 34, and the former have to report annually for a month's training.

Israel has been variously described as a 'melting-pot', a 'pressure-cooker' and a 'social stew', in the sense that all the communities with their different languages and customs, which have come into Israel since 1948, are being blended into one homogeneous whole. This would be unfortunate if it were true, but it isn't. The inclination to blend is not strong, nor are the opportunities so numerous, but the army is one unavoidable meeting point. It helps to induce a sense of unity; it gives an education to many immigrants who received none in their childhood; it inculcates a knowledge of Hebrew which might otherwise have been slowly acquired or not acquired at all. The army is the premier adult educational establish-ment in the country.

The Jews have always put a high premium on education, but they can be too insistent as to exactly what type of education they want, and this naturally breeds factionalism.

During the Mandate and up to 1953 there were three major groups in the Jewish educational system: the General, i.e. non-political schools, which included the Herzlia Gymnasium in Tel-Aviv and the Reali school in Haifa (the two with the highest reputation in the country); the Labour schools, which were operated by the Histadrut; and the religious schools run by the Mizrachi. All three groups were nominally under the control of the Vaad Leumi, but all were jealous of their autonomy, and apart from the waste which such multiplication involved, party interests could be made to override pedagogical ones, and the children suffered.

In 1953, in the face of opposition from the communists, Mapam and Aguda, the government decided to establish a unified system of state education. The attempt did not pass without its inevitable political crisis. On 25 May General Zionist members of the coalition resigned after some former Labour schools insisted on flying the Red Flag on May Day. In the Bill which eventually became law, only the Israel flag was allowed in schools. It provided for the standardization of 75 per cent of the curricula of all schools, while the remaining 25 per cent could follow any trend – subject to the agreement of the Ministry of Education – desired by the majority of parents of children in any particular school. The ultra-Orthodox Aguda, not satisfied with this, opted out of the state system and continues to run its own schools, though the state covers 85 per cent of its budget.

Primary education is free and compulsory between the ages of 5 and 14.

Secondary schools charge fees ranging from about £100 to £125 a year, but there are numerous bursaries given by the Ministry of Education and local authorities, and about half of the 52,000 children in secondary schools receive their education free.[44]

Higher education is the one sphere of Jewish life which has been comparatively – though not entirely – free of party imbroglios. The oldest higher education establishment is the Israel Institute of Technology, Haifa, which has produced most of the applied scientists and civil engineers working in Israel today. At the end of the Mandate it had 678 students. Today it has 3,250 undergraduates, 1,100 post-graduate students and an academic staff of 425 working in 14 faculties.

The foundation stone of the Hebrew University was laid on Mt Scopus in 1918, 'a great act of faith', as Weizmann called it, and the University was formally opened by Arthur Balfour in 1925.

The University area was cut off from the rest of Israel by the War of Liberation, and the University buildings, together with the old Hadassah hospital, remained derelict until the Old City was recaptured by the Jews in 1967. For a number of years the University was scattered among convents, schools and offices all round Jerusalem, till it moved to a permanent home on Givat Ram, near the newly built Knesset, the Hakirya (Israel's Whitehall), and the National Museum. Today it has over 12,000 undergraduate and post-graduate students, including over 800 medical and dental students.

Tel-Aviv, which until recently accommodated a number of departments of the Hebrew University, made a bid for autonomy in 1964 and now has a large campus in the northern suburb of Ramat Aviv, with 3,000 students and an academic staff of 444.

Bar Ilan University at Ramat Gan, near Tel-Aviv, is a religious university, but is not in any sense a theological college. Theology, indeed, is one subject which it does not and cannot teach, for to the Orthodox Jew the very idea of theology is mildly heretical, presuming as it does to examine the credentials of God.

The University has some 2,000 students and a teaching staff of 350, and runs courses in the humanities, social sciences and natural science. Its speciality is a comprehensive course in Jewish studies, but it tries to infuse into all its studies something of the spirit of Jewish tradition.

Beersheba, in the south, now has a University College, and Haifa, apart from the growing humanities faculty of its Technion, is planning to build a major university.

There are also 187 Yeshivoth in Israel, with about 15,000 students, most of them concentrated in Jerusalem. Yeshivoth (singular: Yeshiva) are institutes for devotional studies, which does not mean that they are Rabbinical seminars, even though many of their students do emerge with Rabbinical qualifications and take up employment as Rabbis or teachers. They are uniquely Jewish institutions, and they exist not to offer professional qualifications, but to imbue their students with *Ahavat Torah*, a love for the Torah.

At the apex of the higher educational system stands the Weizmann Institute of Science, which grew out of the Daniel Sieff Research Institute founded in Rehovoth in 1934, and renamed in honour of Chaim Weizmann ten years later.

About 300 scientists, some of them of world rank, are at work on over 200 research projects in 19 different departments. The Institute also includes the Feinberg Graduate School in the Natural Sciences with 260 students.

The Weizmann Institute is the pride of Israel, and in August 1960 it was host to an international conference on 'The Role of Sciences in the Advancement of New States'. The participants included scientists and statesmen from all over the world, among them Sir John Cockcroft, Professor P. M. S. Blackett and the Prime Ministers of the Congo, Chad and Nepal.

Israel is a small densely populated country and it regards its population as its greatest natural resource. It has lavished every penny its strained economy would allow on its educational institutions – as well as a rich flow of funds from Jewish communities overseas – but it is by no means clear that it has employment opportunities for all the talent it produces, and in fact a great many of its graduates go abroad, and many of them stay abroad.

Israel is particularly rich in artistic talent, which finds expression in many ways. There are numerous theatre companies, of which the best known are the Habimah, Israel's National Theatre, founded in Russia in 1918 and brought over to Palestine ten years later; the Ohel, or the workers' theatre, founded in 1925; and the Kameri Theatre, the least inhibited of the three, founded in 1944. There is also a theatre in Haifa, founded six years ago, sponsored by the municipality.

The classics enjoy steady support, though recent productions have also included Hebrew versions of Harold Pinter's *Birthday Party*, Edward Albee's *Who's Afraid of Virginia Woolf?*, Bertolt Brecht's *Mother Courage*, Arnold Wesker's *Chips With Everything*, James Baldwin's *Blues for Mr Charlie*, and *My Fair Lady*. Indigenous productions have not been numerous nor, with the exception of Nathan Alterman's *King Solomon and the Cobbler*, particularly successful.[45]

In the field of music there are 25 musical conservatoires in Israel, with some 9,000 students. The Israel Philharmonic Orchestra, founded by Bronislaw Hubermann in 1936, is among the leading orchestras in the world, and has a large and devoted following of over 27,000 subscribers. Its permanent home is the huge, modernistic 3,000seat Frederic Mann auditorium in TelAviv. About a third of its 104 players were born in Israel or trained there.

There are numerous dancing groups, the best known of which is the Inbal Dance Theatre, founded in 1949 to preserve the folk art of Yemenite Jews.

The Israel Museum opened in 1965, and sited on a hill top near the Hebrew University, includes the Bezalel Museum, with its large collection of Jewish folk art, founded in 1906; the Billy Rose Art Garden of modern sculpture; the Solomon Bronfman Biblical and Archaeological Museum; and the Shrine of the Book which contains seven Dead Sea Scrolls, and some letters of BarKochba (leader of a Jewish rising against Rome in the second century AD), which were unearthed in the Judean desert in 1959.

The hunger for reading matter is incessant and it is not quite satisfied by the country's 1,000 libraries and their 8,000,000 books, and its numerous publishing houses producing over 2,000 titles a year.

The Hebrew Authors' Association founded in 1921 has about 300 members, very few of whom, however, can derive a livelihood from their writing, and it is not uncommon to hear complaints that the Israel public prefers translations of foreign classics or, worse, foreign trash, to the work of its own writers. Many households, however, contain the collected works of Israel's bestknown writer, the enigmatic Shmuel Yosef Agnon, and those that did not, rapidly acquired a set after he won the Nobel Prize in 1966.

The limitation from which every Israel writer suffers is that he is dealing with a small public not all of whom can read or understand Hebrew.

The fanatical devotion of Eliezer Ben Yehuda (1858–1922)[46] and others to the revival of the Hebrew language, though it achieved a miracle, could not altogether avoid the babel of tongues resulting from mass immigration – Yiddish, Polish and Russian in the twenties, German in the thirties, Romanian, Hungarian and Arabic after the war. The children could acquire their Hebrew in the schools, the young people in the army, but the older arrivals naturally stuck to the tongue they knew best, and in spite of a long drawn-out war which at one time was fought by the devotees of Hebrew against Yiddish, this bastard tongue, compounded of German, Hebrew, Russian and terms acquired from every place of Jewish sojournment has shown remarkable powers of persistence.

The government, the Jewish Agency, the Histadrut have made concerted efforts to teach adult newcomers Hebrew, and there are today some 74 Ulpanim running intensive Hebrew courses for over 8,000 adult students.

The babel of tongues, however, though diminished, remains, and of Israel's 25 daily papers (23 morning, and 2 evening), 9 are in foreign languages including English, German, Arabic, Hungarian, French, Polish, Yiddish, Bulgarian and Romanian. The two evening papers, *Maariv* and *Yediot Aharanoth*, are both independent and this is perhaps one of the reasons why they are the two most popular papers in the country, with the former enjoying a circulation of nearly 100,000.

The oldest and most influential of the morning papers, *Haaretz*, with a policy veering towards right of centre, is independent, but most of the other papers are tied – some of them hand and foot – to the political parties.

The language of political debate in the press is outspoken in the extreme and a libel law is under consideration which, it is hoped, will check the excesses without seriously impeding the freedom of debate.

Israel has largely maintained the municipal structure, though, of course, in a much extended form, inherited from the Mandate, and the judicial system also owes much to the British pattern.

At the apex of the system is the Supreme Court, in Jerusalem, which is composed of a President, Permanent Deputy President and 8 Justices. Beneath it are 4 district courts in Jerusalem, Tel-Aviv (which is divided into a criminal and civil division), Haifa (which also functions as an Admiralty court), and Beersheba.

At the base are 25 Magistrates Courts.

The last-mentioned deal with minor misdemeanours, and civil claims under the value of IL3,000. The District Courts deal with all civil and criminal matters not within the jurisdiction of the Magistrates Courts, and may hear appeals against the latter's decisions.

The Supreme Court acts as a Court of Appeal, and also as a High Court dealing with matters outside the jurisdiction of other Courts or tribunals. It may make orders for the release of persons unlawfully detained, or to public authorities where their action or inaction has infringed the law, or to other tribunals to restrain themselves within the limits of their jurisdiction.

There are also 19 Rabbinical Courts and their equivalents in the other religious communities, which have jurisdiction on matters of personal status such as marriage, divorce, alimony, wills and probate, custody of children, paternity and adoption. They may, given the agreement of both parties, also hear civil suits.

The important powers enjoyed by the religious courts in a community which is largely non-religious and in some cases anti-religious have led to considerable civil unrest and more than one political crisis.[47]

Israel is overwhelmingly a country of road users.

The 471 miles of railway, including recent extensions from Lydda to Beersheba and from Beersheba to Dimona, account for under 5 per cent of traffic receipts.

There were in January 1965 over 152,000 vehicles in Israel, that is, one to every 16 people, and 43 (compared to 23 in 1960) to every kilometre of highway.

Buses carry four out of every five passengers in the country. Seating capacity has gone up from 85,000 in 1960 to 124,000 in 1965. The two bus cooperatives, Egged and Dan, account for 95 per cent of the traffic.

The number of taxis in Israel has been virtually constant since 1956, especially in the main urban centres, though licences have been granted to operators in the new development areas. Even then the number has only increased from 2,465 in 1959 to 2,500 at the end of 1964. Of that number, 400 are engaged in inter-urban sherut services, which follow the bus routes and may pick up and deposit passengers (who pay only for their one seat) all along the routes. There are urban sherut taxis, which are only a little more expensive to use than buses, but they are only a little more comfortable, and not much quicker. More than 80 per cent of freight in the country goes by road. Half of the 35,000 trucks in use are more than ten years old.

In 1964 police ordered 2,331 vehicles off the road after finding them mechanically defective. There were 380,150 traffic offences during the same period, 16,000 people injured (over a third of them pedestrians) and 325 people (including 56 children) killed. The casualty figures represent increases of 13 per cent and 14 per cent respectively over the previous year. The use of the roads in Israel can be a nerve-racking experience.

Shipping, with the help of vessels built with German reparations, has expanded dramatically, too dramatically in fact for the state of the market. The Israel merchant fleet has grown from 4 ships, of about 6,000 tons dead weight, in 1958, to 90 ships and a capacity of 933,522 tons in 1964. There were also 14 ships, totalling 350,000 tons, under construction, including 3 refrigerated vessels (27,000 tons), 4 bulk carriers (195,000), 4 coastal freighters (12,000), 2 tankers (121,000) and a car ferry (7,000).

Israel had obviously entertained hopes of becoming an important sea-carrier, and deriving considerable foreign revenue therefrom. Instead she derived serious losses and recently she has been forced to dispose of a number of vessels, including the 24,500-ton S.S. *Shalom*, flagship of the Zim line.

Civil aviation, if less ambitious, has had a happier record. El Al Israel National Airlines currently has a fleet of 2 Britannias and 5 707 and 720 Boeings – an investment of $40,000,000. The number of its flights has increased from 639 in 1958-9 to 1,423 in 1964-5 and its flying hours from 13,840 to 19,228. El Al flew 13,000,000 kilometres in 1964 and carried nearly 230,000 passengers.

Arkia airlines operates internal air services from Tel-Aviv to Beersheba, Eilat, Haifa, Rosh Pina in Galilee, and Masada in the Negev.

Jaffa, the ancient port of the Holy Land, is now closed.

Haifa, the main port, together with its auxiliary harbour at the mouth of the Kishon river, can handle up to 3,000,000 tons of cargo a year. Its installations include a 10,000-ton floating dock and a grain silo with an intake of 480 tons an hour.

Ashdod, Israel's second deep-water port, came into use at the end of 1965 and can handle about 1,000,000 tons of cargo a year. Deepening operations should increase its capacity four-fold by 1970.

Eilat, Israel's outlet in the Red Sea, which, as a port, was hardly more than a gesture of defiance till 1956, has grown enormously since. It handled over 200,000 tons of cargo in 1964, and its capacity was enlarged by the opening of a new harbour in September 1965, and there are plans to extend it further.[48]

6   Politics and parliament

UNTIL THE END OF THE MANDATE the internal affairs of the Yishuv had, as we have seen, been handled by the Vaad Leumi, and the external ones by the Jewish Agency. On 15 May 1948 the former disappeared, and the executive of the latter virtually became the provisional government of the new state. Ben Gurion, who had been Chairman of the one, became Prime Minister of the other; Moshe Sharett, the Political Secretary, became Foreign Minister; Eliezer Kaplan, the Treasurer, became Finance Minister, and so on. Some of the less senior offices, however, were occupied by individuals from outside the Agency. Mr Shitrit, the Minister of Police, for example, had been a district magistrate, and I. M. Levin, the Minister without Portfolio, was from the ultra-Orthodox Aguda party which had always kept itself apart from the Zionist groups.

The Jewish Agency did not vanish. Its role, however, was altered and today it is concerned mainly with encouraging the immigration of Jews to Israel, their reception on arrival, and their absorption into the economy. It also functions as a sort of second-eleven government from which some individuals may be promoted to the first eleven, and to which others may be relegated. Mr Levi Eshkol, for example, was Treasurer of the Jewish Agency till he became Minister of Finance, and the late Moshe Sharett became Chairman of the Jewish Agency after he resigned from the government. One observer has described the Jewish Agency as Israel's House of Lords.[49]

The overriding concern of the new government was, as we have seen, the military one, but even while the fighting was at its height, machinery was being prepared for the first General Election. And fighting or no fighting, each party struggled for the largest share of the vote. On this front at least there has never been any truce.

On 25 January 1949, a little over a fortnight after the cease-fire, Israel went to the polls for the first time. One hundred and twenty members were elected to its Constituent Assembly, the Knesset. It has no Upper Chamber.

Israel is a Republic headed by a President who is elected by a simple majority of the Knesset for a period of five years and who may if he wishes be re-elected. His function is largely akin to that of a constitutional monarch. He signs international treaties, receives ambassadors and visiting heads of state, and may exercise the prerogative of pardon. During a political crisis he will intervene to obtain a settlement.

Israel's first President was Dr Chaim Weizmann, a man of undefined political sympathies who was generally looked on as being above party. He was succeeded on his death in 1952 by Itzhak Ben Zvi, who arrived in Palestine with the Second Aliya and who, with Ben Gurion, helped to build up the Jewish labour movement, the Histadrut, and Mapai. Ben Zvi was at one time a Chairman and President of the Vaad Leumi and was a member of the first and second Knesset, and author of numerous works on Eastern Jewish communities. He was succeeded on his death in 1963 by the present head of State, President Zalman Shazar, who was editor of the Histadrut daily *Davar* from 1925 to 1949 and Minister of Education from 1949 to 1951.

Israel has no written constitution and the powers of the Knesset are substantially those of the British House of Commons. It is the supreme authority, and its legislation may not be questioned in the courts. It is elected for four years, and it alone may dissolve itself before that period has expired. In this respect it is even stronger than the House of Commons, though in practice, if a government has resigned and no successor can be found, it would have no alternative but to enter into dissolution.

All men and women in Israel over the age of 18 are able to vote, and all over 21 may stand for election, which is based on a system of proportional representation. In 1949 no less than 21 parties submitted lists and 12 secured one or more seats.

The largest political party, and the one round which every government since the creation of the state has been formed, is the Israel Labour Party, Mapai.

Mifleget Poalei Eretz Yisrael, to give it its full name, resulted from the fusion of various labour groups in 1930, and it soon came to dominate the National Council of the Yishuv, the Vaad Leumi, as well as the Zionist Congress. Its position in Congress gave its representatives the leading offices on the Executive of the Jewish Agency, and seats in the provisional government.

The 1949 elections confirmed them in office. Mapai received nearly 36 per cent of the vote and 46 out of the 120 seats.

Mapai is socialist, but pragmatic rather than doctrinaire, and its economic and foreign policies are determined by prevailing cir-cumstances. It is thus in many ways akin to the British Labour Party. It believes in a planned economy, and if one can find no references to nationalization in its programme, it is because it already controls 'the commanding heights of the economy' through the Histadrut. Nor is it particularly concerned with the re-distribution of wealth, partly because there is little wealth to re-distribute, but largely because the Jewish society which has evolved in Israel is an egalitarian one, and wages are dependent on needs as well as skills and the pull of the market. Egalitarian principles have been receding a little, but a university porter with a large family may still earn more than a university don with a small one.

Mapai would have wished Israel to have a place among the unaligned nations of the world, but the unfriendly attitude of the USSR, together with Israel's dependence on the United States, have pushed it towards the Western camp.

Second in the 1949 elections came Mapam, the United Workers' Party, with nearly 15 per cent of the vote and 19 seats.

Mapam stands well to the left of Mapai and draws its strength and prestige from the kibbutz movement. It is neo-Marxist, and like Mapai believes in a controlled economy, only its controls would be more widespread and stringent, and it would nationalize the natural resources of the country and its key industries. It was formed in 1948 from a union between Ahdut Avoda, which had been fretting on

89

the left wing of Mapai and had finally broken away in 1944, and Hashomer Hatzair.

Mapam has striven for Jewish-Arab working-class solidarity and has endeavoured both in the Knesset and outside to improve the conditions of Israel's Arabs. It would have liked a pro-Soviet, or at least what it calls a 'neutralist' foreign policy, but it has been embarrassed by the virulent anti-Zionism of the Communist bloc.

Third in the 1949 elections came the Religious Bloc, with about 12 per cent of the vote and 16 seats. The Bloc was an *ad hoc* union of two other unions, and consisted of the Mizrachi and Hapoel Hamizrachi, the Agudas Yisrael and the Poalei Agudas Yisrael.

In the same way as all labour groups are socialist, only some more socialist than others, all the religious groups are religious, only the Aguda pair are more so than the Mizrachi pair. They divide on social and economic issues, with Aguda and Mizrachi to the right, and Poalei Aguda and Hapoel Hamizrachi to the left.

The Aguda pair believe in a theocracy based on the Torah, so that there would be a virtual upper chamber of Rabbis which could veto all legislation not in accordance with the Torah. On the other hand, the Mizrachi pair, which have since fused, take a more realistic view of the function of religion in the state and would like legislation to be guided by Torah principles. Unlike the Aguda, they have been willing to compromise on certain issues, like the conscription of women. Unlike it also, the Mizrachi pair have always been an integral part of the Zionist movement, while the Aguda have kept themselves apart.

Herut (the Freedom Party) came fourth with 11·5 per cent of the votes and 14 seats. Herut is the largest of the right-wing groups and is the reincarnation of the old Revisionist movement founded by Jabotinsky which in its turn had given birth to the Irgun Tzvai Leumi. It was to nationalism what Aguda is to religion, rigid and uncompromising, but its demands for the recovery of the whole of Palestine, including Transjordan, have been little heard of lately, and it has been less chauvinistic. Today it is an almost sober right-wing party, calling for the limitation of state intervention in the economy, improved facilities for investors, the fairer spread of taxation, and greater scope for free enterprise. It is now part of a new group called the Gahal, of which we shall hear more later.

The General Zionists, which came fifth with 5·2 per cent of the poll and 7 seats, has always been the party of the centre supported by large and small manufacturers and entrepreneurs. It is now also part of Gahal.

The Progressive Party, which came next with some 4 per cent of the votes and 5 seats, formed the liberal party. It consists of professional men and intellectuals and draws its strength largely from the wave of immigrants from Germany and central Europe who settled in Palestine in the 1930s and who later formed the New Immigration Party. Though small, it is respected and influential.

The Communist Party gained 3·5 per cent of the votes and 4 seats, and the Arab parties 3 per cent of the votes and 2 seats. A large part of the communist vote is Arab and it represents a protest vote rather than support for Marxism.

After the polls Ben Gurion hoped to form a national coalition composed of all the parties in the provisional government, but Mapam wanted the Ministry of Defence, with which he had no intention of parting, and the General Zionists wanted a number of portfolios out of proportion to their strength in the Knesset. His coalition, therefore, consisted of Mapai, which had 7 members; the Religious Bloc, 3; the Progressives, 1, and the Sephardim, 1.

Ben Gurion was born in Plonsk, Poland, in 1886 and settled in Palestine 20 years later. He was one of the pioneers of the Second Aliya, and worked as a labourer in the vineyards of Rishon Le Zion and the orange groves of Petach Tikva, and as a ploughman at Serjera in Galilee.

'No shopkeepers here', he wrote to his father, shortly after his arrival, 'or speculators, no non-Jewish hirelings, no idlers living on the labour of others.'[50] This ideal of self-labour was fundamental to the Jewish pioneer, and to the new Jewish society evolving in Palestine. Another was self-defence, and with the help of Itzhak Ben Zvi and other contemporaries of the Second Aliya, he helped to found the Hashomer defence corps.

In 1910 Ben Gurion was wooed by Ben Zvi to Jerusalem to become editor of a weekly Hebrew Labour paper *Ha'achdut*, and left three years later to study law in Constantinople, where he was eventually joined at the Ottoman University School of Law by Ben Zvi and Moshe Shertok. His studies were interrupted by the outbreak of the First World War. He returned to Palestine and then made his way to New York where he became a corporal in the American battalion of the Jewish Legion.

After the war Ben Gurion returned to the labour movement and in 1920 he was instrumental in creating the General Federation of Labour, the Histadrut, and became its General Secretary. Ten years later he brought a number of Palestine labour groups together to form Mapai, and became head of the new party. It won control of the Vaad Leumi and in 1933 it became the largest party at the Zionist Congress. In 1936 he became Chairman of the Jewish Agency Executive, in which capacity he attended the St James's Conference in London in 1939.

The White Paper which followed the Conference impaired the standing of Weizmann in the Zionist movement. His policy of moderation, his unceasing faith in Britain, seemed to yield nothing but disappointment. Ben Gurion, who was never a preacher of moderation, came to the fore. He formulated the Biltmore programme, and had it endorsed by the Zionist General Council. He gave Zionism a new tempo, a new militancy.

While Weizmann directed negotiations in London and Washington, Ben Gurion led the home front, defied the British limitations on immigration, built up the Hagana and prepared the Yishuv for what he saw as the inevitable war with the Arabs.

If Weizmann with his patrician manner, urbanity and charm was a diplomat of the old school, Ben Gurion, craggy, tempestuous and truculent was in a school of his own. When he arrived in London in 1946 to demand 100,000 immigration certificates for Jews in the displaced persons' camps, the Colonial Secretary complained that his manner 'was different from anything which I had ever experienced', but it reflected the temper of the Yishuv. The pre-war days of Havlaga, restraint, were over.

20 Under the chairmanship
of David Ben Gurion the
National Council met on 15
May 1948 and the state of
Israel, based on the precepts of
liberty, justice and peace, was
proclaimed.

21 One year later on
12 May 1949 Israel was
elected a member of the United
Nations and her flag was
hoisted at UN Headquarters,
Lake Success, New York.

22 One of the earliest settlements in Israel was Kiryat Gat, established in 1923. This is the railway station.

23 In 1909 a gathering had met at the Hill of Spring to discuss the creation of Tel-Aviv which was to become the largest city in Israel.

24 These families of early settlers celebrate the feast of the first ripe fruits at
Ain Harod.

25 Good irrigation of land was essential to the welfare of the early settlers. This
photograph of the 1920's shows the building of a reservoir in the Valley of Kishon.

26 The kibbutz or collective settlement is basic to the economy of Israel.
This is a kibbutz named Mayan Baruch and reflects much of the spirit of these
early pioneers.

27 The first immigrants to pour into the country often had to make do with
primitive conditions, such as this camp inhabited by Jews from North Africa.

28 Immigrants arriving at Haifa.

29 (*left below*) Families who have been separated by war and are lucky to have survived are reunited in their homeland.

30 (*right below*) An immigrant from North America.

31 The backbone of the Jewish state is the kibbutz movement, a network of cooperative settlements spread across the country. *Above*, a procession at Kibbutz Ginnegar during the Festival of the First Fruits.

32 The kibbutz is basically an agricultural enterprise. Haymaking by members of a kibbutz in the Shanon Valley, near Lydda.

33 The granary at Kibbutz Hanita on the Lebanon-Israel frontier. Such border
settlements were defence posts in war. The murals on the wall, typical of many
kibbutzim, depict scenes of the Jewish Exile in Egypt.

34 The first kibbutz founded in 1909 was at Degania in the north of Israel.
All property is collectively owned.

35 In 1921 the first Moshav was established at Nahala, seen here from the air.
Each member of a Moshav works in his own plot of land and keeps any
surplus money he may earn.

7   The road to Sinai

IN 1949 THE MAIN CONCERN of the newly installed administration, as of every succeeding one, was defence. Next in priority – and the two are not wholly unconnected – was immigration. Some 11,000 internees kept in Cyprus until the end of the Mandate were brought over almost at once, and priority was also given to Jews still living in displaced persons' camps in Germany. In the first seven and a half months of statehood over 100,000 immigrants came in, and a further 240,000 arrived the following year.

The ArabJewish conflict seriously affected the position of the oriental Jewish communities, most of whom had been living in comparative amity with their Moslem neighbours, and a great many felt compelled to leave and settle in Israel. There had been a trickle of Yemeni Jews to the Holy Land from the earliest times, and in 1950 the entire community of 50,000 was transferred to Israel by the airborne operation 'Magic Carpet'.[51] Most of Iraqi Jewry was also evacuated, and there were large movements of population from Morocco, Tunisia, Egypt and Turkey. Most of what was left of Polish Jewry emigrated to Israel during 1950–1, as well as a large part of Romanian Jewry. During those two years nearly 350,000 newcomers arrived in Israel. By the end of 1951 its Jewish population had doubled.

Such an increase brought appalling economic and social problems. A sizeable part of the cabinet was involved in yearly fundraising missions to the Jewish communities of America, Britain and South Africa. They gave generously, but not enough to cover the long-term or even short-term needs of the country. In 1951 Ben Gurion launched a Bonds-for-Israel drive in the United States, which brought in $651,325,000 during the next 12 years.

In March 1951 Israel submitted a claim for $1,500,000,000 to Germany in reparations for losses suffered by Jews at the hands of the Nazis. The move aroused fierce opposition from both the extreme left and the extreme right, and over 100 policemen were injured in the most violent demonstrations Israel had yet seen. The government persevered and as a result of the agreement negotiated with West Germany, Israel has received some $820,000,000 in reparations.

Most of the newcomers, especially from the oriental countries, arrived without capital or skills, and some 10 per cent of the adults were too old or disabled to be employable.[52] In 1949 and 1950 new arrivals were housed in the towns and villages abandoned by the Arabs, but after that a critical housing shortage developed, and *maabarot*, transit camps, were established to accommodate them. New villages were built and whole areas developed. By the end of 1951 the 125,000 acres under cultivation at the end of the Mandate had grown to 850,000 acres; 15 new agricultural settlements had been established near the borders with Syria, Jordan and Egypt; the number in industry and crafts grew from 80,000 to nearly 120,000; there was a large number of men employed on housing and civil engineering projects. But even then the expansion could not keep pace with the rising population. There was serious overcrowding. Severe unemployment was avoided, but the continuous pumping of credit into the economy and the financing of part of the defence budget by a cascade of Treasury Bills, accelerated the rate of inflation. Exports for the years 1949 and 1950 totalled £23,622,000. Imports were about eight times as high.

The government, which was shaken by a minor crisis at the end of 1950, fell in February 1951. The cause, as in numerous later crises, was religion. Most of the new immigrants arriving from oriental countries were Orthodox Jews. The individuals in charge of the reception centres were usually not. The members of the Religious Bloc insisted that the children of such immigrants should be given a religious education. When they could not get their way they withdrew from the coalition and it collapsed.

The Knesset, after little more than two years of life, was dissolved and new elections were held in July. Mapai made some slight gains; Mapam suffered slight losses. Herut, however, lost 6 of its 14 seats, and the General Zionists increased their contingent from 7 to 20. This was the most dramatic result of the election. Part of the Herut loss was no doubt the General Zionists' gain, but many voters were also becoming restless with the severe rationing, shortages and controls.

The Religious Bloc came to the electorate in two parts, Mizrachi/ Hapoel Hamizrachi and Aguda/Poalei Aguda and between them they got one seat less than in the previous election. This was a severe disappointment. The electorate had nearly doubled, and as the great majority of newcomers were Orthodox it was thought that the religious vote would rise dramatically. That it fell was in part due to the fact that many of the newcomers tended to look to Ben Gurion as their saviour and their vote for Mapai was an expression of their gratitude.

Ben Gurion invited all parties save the communists and Herut to enter into a new coalition and negotiations continued until October. In the end he reached agreement on basic terms only with the religious parties, and his new cabinet was not distinctly different from the old.

During 1952 immigration declined to 23,357, and in 1953 to 10,347 and the pressure on the economy eased a little. The reception camps were cleared. Rationing of food, clothing, household goods and building materials was abolished. The flourishing black market collapsed.

The new government had not been in office a year when it was shaken by another crisis. The issue again was religion. Under the National Service Bill Ben Gurion, after pressure from all the religious parties, had agreed that girls who objected to military service on religious grounds could be directed for duty in agriculture, hospitals or immigration camps. Aguda and Poalei Aguda objected even to this and withdrew from the coalition. On this occasion Ben Gurion was able to bring the General Zionists into the government by giving them the Ministries of the Interior, Health, Communications, Commerce and Industry, and agreeing to a freer economy.

Chaim Weizmann, who had done possibly even more than Herzl to make the dream of a Jewish state a reality, died on 9 November 1952. He had been in failing health since the end of the war, but would have wished for a more active role than his office allowed him. He was succeeded as President by Itzhak Ben Zvi.

In November 1953 Ben Gurion suddenly announced that he was about to resign. He had been at the helm of Jewish affairs since 1936 and he felt he needed a rest. He resigned a month later and joined Kibbutz Sde Boker, in the Negev. He was succeeded by his Foreign Minister, Moshe Sharett.

Sharett was born in the Ukraine in 1894 and arrived in Palestine in his early childhood with the Second Aliya. He studied at the University of Constantinople and held commissioned rank in the Turkish army during the First World War. After the war he was a student at the London School of Economics. When Chaim Arlosoroff[53] was assassinated in 1933 he succeeded him as head of the political department of the Jewish Agency, and distinguished himself as a negotiator and debater during the League of Nations hearings on Palestine.

Sharett's cabinet was much like its predecessor and based on the same party alignments. But there was one important change. Ben Gurion had retained the Premiership and the Ministry of Defence. Sharett divested himself of the latter office and gave it to Pinchas Lavon, with consequences which we shall notice later.

The new government, Sharett told the Knesset, 'regards itself as a direct continuation of the previous government and remains faithful to the basic principles presented by the previous Prime Minister'. But it differed in one important respect: it was less aggressive.

The various armistice agreements signed in 1949 had brought imperfect peace to Israel. There were small sporadic frontier incidents in 1949 and 1950. In 1951 they became more serious and less sporadic and in that year they resulted in the death or injury of 137 Israelis. In the following year there were 147 casualties.

Most of the casualties occurred on or near the frontier with Jordan and Israel replied to attack with counter-attack. The United Nations had established a Truce Supervisory Organization in Palestine, and Mixed Armistice Commissions to investigate violations of the armistice agreement, but they could not stop the incidents, which grew in frequency and scale. In August 1952 the Israeli conscription period was extended from two years to thirty months.

In the period January to October 1953, 40 Israelis were killed on the Jordan border, 79 wounded and 23 taken prisoner. On the night of 12–13 October of the same year an Israeli woman and her two small children, in a village near the Jordan border, were killed by a hand grenade.

On the following night a force of about 500 armed Israelis crossed the Jordan frontier and attacked the village of Quibya, killing at least 42 civilians, wounding 15 others, and destroying houses, a school and the local reservoir.

An emergency meeting of the local Mixed Armistice Commission condemned 'the cold-blooded murder' of the villagers, and Britain, America and France called for a special meeting of the Security Council to discuss the Israel-Arab frontier situation. On 24 November the Council expressed 'the strongest censure' of the Quibya raid, and called on Israel 'to take effective measures to prevent all such actions in the future'.

For the next three months all was comparatively quiet, then, on 17 March 1954, an Israeli bus travelling through the southern Negev was ambushed and raked with machine-gun fire. Eleven passengers were killed and two seriously injured. There was no retaliatory action. Israel complained to the Mixed Armistice Commission, and when the Chairman refused to condemn Jordan because he felt the evidence was inconclusive, the Israeli delegation withdrew from the Commission.

In September the situation on the Egyptian border began to deteriorate, and during the autumn and winter there were over 20 Egyptian incursions into Israeli territory, most of them minor, but leading altogether to the death of 7 Israelis and the wounding of 24, as well as numerous acts of sabotage. These were condemned by the Israel-Egypt Mixed Armistice Commission. There were no Israeli reprisals. On 21 February 1955, Ben Gurion emerged from retire-ment to become Defence Minister. On 28 February an Israeli force crossed into the Gaza strip, demolished a military post and water-pumping station, killed 38 Egyptians and wounded 31 others. Israeli casualties were 8 dead and 13 wounded. The attack was condemned by both the MAC and the Security Council. The latter made the usual appeals to both sides to abide by the armistice agreement, which were wholly without effect.

The Arab infiltrators dug deeper and deeper into Israeli territory, penetrating on one occasion as far as Rehovot, 25 miles south of Tel-Aviv, and it soon became clear that they were trained com-mandos – *Fedayeen*, as the Arabs called them – following a prescribed pattern of terror.

This external threat was not sufficient to maintain internal unity. In June 1955 the government was charged with interfering with the independence of the judiciary, after the Attorney General had appealed to the Supreme Court to quash a District Court ruling in a libel action affecting a senior civil servant who was also a member of Mapai. Motions of no confidence were tabled by Herut and the communists. The General Zionists, the second largest party in the coalition, abstained from the vote. The Prime Minister Moshe Sharett thereupon resigned and a month later new elections were held.

There were changes in the party list. Mapam, the pro-Soviet, neo-Marxist party, had been torn apart by the anti-Jewish purges in the Soviet Union culminating in the alleged 'doctors' plot' on the lives of the Soviet leaders, and the attacks on Zionists as 'executors of the State Department's espionage operations within the Soviet Union', and as 'enemies of the Jewish workers'. Three months earlier 11 Czechoslovak Jews were indicted and found guilty as 'Trotskyist-Titoist-Zionist-bourgeois-nationalist traitors and enemies of the Jewish people', in a trial which was perhaps the worst manifestation of antisemitism the world had seen since the war.

In the face of all this it was difficult for even the most dedicated Jewish socialist to maintain a pro-Soviet stance, and early in 1953 Mapam expelled three leading members, Dr Moshe Sneh (a former head of the Hagana), Dr Abraham Berman, and Pinchas Tubin, who had tried to justify the attitude of the Soviet bloc to Zionism. This, however, did not end the dissension in Mapam.

Ahdut Avoda, which had been a wing of Mapai, but found the party too pragmatic and broke away in 1948 to join with Hashomer Hatzair in the formation of Mapam, now found Mapam too Marxist and doctrinaire and broke away to stand as an independent party. (In 1966 it joined in an alignment with Mapai. The prodigal son had all but returned to his home.) In the 1955 election it won 10 seats, one more than Mapam. Mapai lost 4 seats, the General Zionists lost 7, and the religious parties won 2. At the bottom of the list two small parties were knocked out by a change in the electoral law requiring a party to gain at least 1 per cent of the vote to get a seat.

The surprise of the election was the triumph of Herut, which increased its vote from 45,651 to 107,190, and its representation from 8 to 15 seats. It is the most militant of the parties and no one doubted that the external situation played a large part in its success.

Sharett stepped down and returned the premiership to Ben Gurion, while retaining the Foreign Office. Nearly four months passed before a government was brought together, and it consisted of a coalition of Mapai, Ahdut Avoda, Mapam, Mizrachi/Hapoel Hamizrachi (who merged on 9 August to form the National Religious Party) and the Progressives.

In the meantime border incidents continued and the incursions of the Fedayeen grew more audacious.

On the night of 31 August–1 September Israel attacked a police station, Khan Yunis in the Gaza strip, killing 40 Egyptians and wounding 40 others.

On 3 November a pitched battle took place at El Auja, on the Egyptian border, which had been declared a demilitarized zone in the 1949 armistice agreement, and which stood astride one of the main roads to Sinai. The Israelis ejected the Egyptians from the zone, inflicted heavy casualties, and took 49 prisoners and a large quantity of equipment.

The Jordanian border was rarely quiet and there was a spate of incidents on the Syrian border. Both, it seemed, stemmed from the activities of Fedayeen operating from Jordanian and Syrian bases.

Egypt also tightened her blockade of Israeli shipping in spite of a 1951 Security Council resolution requiring her to lift all restrictions on ships using the Suez Canal en route for Israel. In September 1954 a small Israeli freighter, the Bat Galim, which tried to run the blockade, was detained, and its crew arrested. In the Gulf of Aqaba, ships bound for Eilat were shelled by Egyptian batteries as they passed through the Straits of Tiran.

At the end of 1955 Israel became aware of a heavy flow of guns, tanks, aircraft and other military equipment from Czechoslovakia to Egypt.

Under a Tripartite Declaration signed by America, Britain and France in 1950, the three powers had pledged themselves to take action 'both within and outside the United Nations' to prevent violations of the armistice agreements, and to limit the supply of arms to Israel and her neighbours.

The armistice agreements had been continuously flouted by all parties and now the balance of power was also impaired.

This caused anxiety in the West especially as the Egyptians had made it perfectly plain on a number of occasions that they looked upon themselves as in a state of war with Israel. Repeated offers – the last one on his installation as Prime Minister in November 1955 – by Ben Gurion to meet Colonel Nasser or any other Arab ruler to work out a settlement without any prior conditions, were ignored. In the autumn Egypt concluded a military pact with Syria and Saudi Arabia.

The ring round Israel was tightening. On 2 January 1956, she extended her period of National Service from $2\frac{1}{2}$ to $3\frac{1}{2}$ years. Throughout the autumn and winter Israel made frantic efforts to counterbalance the arms flow to Egypt and received sympathetic attention from France which supplied her with light tanks, 24 Mystère IV jet fighters and a quantity of other equipment. On 18

June Moshe Sharett, who had directed Israel's foreign policy since the beginning of the state, resigned and was replaced by the Minister of Labour, Mrs Golda Meir, who shared Ben Gurion's views on the military and political problems facing Israel.

On 26 July Colonel Nasser announced the nationalization of the Suez Canal. Britain (who had withdrawn her last troops from the Canal Zone only two months before) and France joined in strong protests. Both were concerned not only about their stake in the Canal itself, but also the 67,000,000 tons of oil a year which passed through the Suez Canal to Western Europe. Britain in particular felt that the nationalization of the Canal was part of a wider scheme of aggression planned by Colonel Nasser.

In October the matter was brought before the Security Council, and Britain, France and Egypt were able to reach agreement on most issues, but a proposal by the first two that the Canal should be internationalized was vetoed by the Soviet Union.

During the early 1950s America and Britain tried to bring the states lying between Greece and Pakistan into a compact linking the NATO countries to the north and the SEATO countries to the east. Turkey and Pakistan signed a pact in 1954, and in February 1955, in spite of opposition from Nasser, Iraq signed a similar treaty with Turkey which came to be known as the Baghdad Pact.

In December 1955 talks in Amman on the possibility of Jordan's accession to the Baghdad Pact led to riots, the fall of the government, and nearly the fall of the monarchy. In March 1956 King Hussein, in an attempt to appease the rioters, dismissed Glubb Pasha as commander of the Arab Legion. The Jordanian Parliament was dissolved and the subsequent election on 21 October was a triumph for the pro-Nasser and anti-Western elements in the country. On 25 October Egypt, Syria and Jordan formed a Joint Military Command headed by the Egyptian Chief of Staff, Abdel Hakim Amer.

On 29 October Israel invaded Sinai.

8   Sinai and after

SINAI was a lightning victory.

On the morning of 31 October 1956, Ben Gurion was already able to report: 'Israel forces have struck into the heart of Sinai and are more than half way to Suez.'

That same day Britain and France issued a twelve-hour ultimatum requiring both sides to cease fire and withdraw ten miles from the canal. Israel, which was not yet within ten miles of the canal, readily complied. Egypt did not. When the ultimatum expired British and French planes attacked Egyptian airfields and destroyed most of the Egyptian air force on the ground.

The land forces which Egypt had sent eastwards to check the Israeli advance were shattered and withdrew in disarray, leaving a vast quantity of equipment.

An Egyptian destroyer which had tried to bombard Haifa was disabled and captured. On 2 November the Israelis took El Arish and Gaza. On 5 November they cleared the whole western shore of the Gulf of Aqaba and opened the approach to Eilat.

On 2 November the United Nations met in special session and called for a cease-fire. Israel was ordered to withdraw her troops to the 1949 frontiers.

Israel ceased fire, but her troops remained in Sinai and the Gaza strip.

On 7 November Ben Gurion received a note from Marshal Bulganin charging the government of Israel with perpetrating 'a treacherous attack on her neighbours', and 'criminally and irresponsibly playing with the fate of the world and of her own people'.

A note from President Eisenhower, couched in friendlier tones, asked Israel to withdraw from Egyptian territory.

On 23 January 1957, Israel withdrew from the whole of Sinai except Sharm el-Sheikh. She remained in the Gaza strip. She would move from the first, Ben Gurion told the Knesset, when freedom of navigation in the Gulf of Aqaba had been assured, and from the second when she had received guarantees against the renewal of Fedayeen raids. Israel, he said, 'perhaps more than any other country, is interested in strengthening the authority of the United Nations to safeguard peace and international justice', but in 1948 when Israel was attacked by five Arab countries, four of which were members of the United Nations, neither the Security Council nor the General Assembly lifted a finger to help her. She was now helping herself.

But the pressure on Israel continued to build up. There was the threat of UN sanctions. Marshal Bulganin sent a second warning, and America urged her to withdraw 'promptly and unconditionally'. On 1 March, she complied.

The news was greeted in Israel with dismay. There were protests in the Knesset, clashes in the streets and numerous arrests. It seemed so abject a surrender after so magnificent a triumph, but Israel had no alternative, and she had achieved her principal objectives. The main threat to her security which had come from Egypt was stilled; the imbalance of power had been redressed. The incursions of Fedayeen, which had been sapping public morale, were stopped.

Israel had demonstrated once again the capacity of her generals and fighting men.

Navigation in the Gulf of Aqaba was free. Eilat, its hinterland, and the whole Negev could be more fully and more rapidly developed.

An Emergency Force created by the United Nations and stationed in the Gaza strip and Sinai brought peace to the southern frontier. There were to be occasional incidents on the border with Jordan, and frequent ones on that with Syria, but Sinai brought comparative tranquillity to Israel. She could now turn to cultivate her own garden.

During the years 1952–4 the flow of immigrants had been comparatively meagre, but as the former French possessions in North Africa moved towards independence the exodus of their Jewish inhabitants quickened, and between 1955 and 1957 a further 165,000 newcomers entered Israel.

In 1953 important deposits of copper had been found in the southern Negev not far from Eilat, and this had been followed by the discovery of significant quantities of various other minerals in different parts of the Negev including phosphates, iron, manganese, copper, gypsum, felspar and kaolin. The installations of the Palestine Potash Company, which were destroyed during the War of Liberation (as the 1948–9 war is known in Israel), were rebuilt and reactivated by 1953 and in the same year a 50-mile road linking Sodom, the site of the installations, and Beersheba was completed.

In July 1955 the biggest irrigation project yet undertaken in Israel brought water from the Yarkon river, which rises in the Judean hills, to the northern Negev.

In September 1955 important oil deposits were struck at Heletz near Ashkelon on a concession previously held by the Iraq Petroleum Company. The deposits did not prove as rich as was at first hoped. Oil imports from the Persian Gulf which before Sinai had to reach Israel by way of the Cape were now able to come through Eilat. In 1956 an oil pipe-line from Eilat to Beersheba was built. Two years later it was extended to Haifa. Work on draining the Hula swamps in north-east Galilee, which had been acquired by the JNF (The Jewish National Fund, founded in 1901 to acquire and reclaim land in Palestine) as early as 1934, was begun in 1948. Nearly ten years later the task was completed and 15,000 richly fertile acres were ready for the plough.

In 1956 work began on Kiryat Gat as the urban centre of a new development area covering 125,000 acres at Lachish between the Hebron hills and Ashkelon. Today Kiryat Gat has a population of about 16,000, and the villages in the surrounding development area a further 17,000. A more modest development near Afula on a 15,000-acre site now accommodates some 600 families in 10 villages. In 1957 the development was begun of some 25,000 acres in the Adullam area near the approaches to Jerusalem, which will eventually accommodate 650 families. Work is also in progress in the Korazim area north of the Sea of Galilee near the Jordan border. A fifth development project for the Beersheba area is still in the planning stage.

In 1955 a new town, Dimona, was founded by North African immigrants in the Negev between Beersheba and the Dead Sea. It is now the textile centre of the Negev and has a population of about 16,000. Another new town was founded at Arad in 1962 not far from the natural-gas deposits at Rosh Zohar.

The Jew has a natural penchant for the town, especially the large town, and Tel-Aviv, Haifa and Jerusalem have acted as magnets on every succeeding wave of immigrants. This was the case during the Mandate; it has been the case since. The new towns and development schemes were determined only partly by the distribution of natural resources. The government was anxious for social, strategic and political reasons to spread the population over the country as evenly as possible.

Vacant spaces invite intruders; during the War of Liberation every settlement had been a citadel. As recently as 1955 a British Prime Minister suggested a re-drawing of boundaries as part of a peace settlement between Israel and the Arabs.[54] The spread of the population was a way of confirming the frontiers. In 1949 about 48 per cent of the population of Israel lived in the three main cities: the proportion today is 31 per cent.

In October 1958 Israel's population topped the two million mark. Today it stands at about 2,530,000, of whom some 200,000 are Moslems, 55,000 are Christians and 29,000 are Druzes and others. The Arab population of the country has more than doubled since 1948, largely through natural increase, though partly through the admission of relatives under a government scheme for re-uniting Arab families divided by the war. The Jewish population has more than trebled since 1948 and two-thirds of the increase was due to immigration. The low Jewish birth-rate compared to the high Arab one is a cause of concern.

Of the newcomers who arrived in Israel between 1948 and 1962 more than half came from what used to be known as the backward countries of Asia and Africa and are now more euphemistically referred to as the less-developed countries. The former French territories of North Africa which provided a large proportion of the immigrants were not in fact all that backward, but the more prosperous Jews opted for France and those who settled in Israel were generally without possessions or skills.

The Jews from Asian and African countries are loosely referred to as *Sephardim*, descendants of the Jews expelled from Spain, which most of them certainly are not. The Jews from European countries are referred to, with similar inaccuracy, as *Ashkenazim*, that is, Germans.

The beginnings of the Zionist movement coincided with the ascendancy of Europe in world affairs, and it was the Ashkenazim who were the pioneers of the First, Second and Third Aliya, who built Petach Tikva and Rishon Le Zion, who drained the swamps, established the kibbutzim and built up a self-defence corps. Of the 500,000 or so Jews who settled in Palestine between 1882 and 1948 only some 10 per cent stemmed from Sephardic communities. It was natural, therefore, that other things being equal the Ashkenazim would have the top jobs, be accommodated in the most attractive quarters, enjoy a more cosseted existence. But other things weren't equal. The Sephardim in most cases had not had the same opportunity to acquire an education, skill or capital, and thus when they settled in Israel they found themselves in the less attractive jobs, in the less comfortable parts of the country, or the less salubrious quarters of the towns. And whenever there was a recession they tended to be the first out of work.

They began to feel that they were 'the hewers of wood and drawers of water' of Israel. They complained of discrimination. There were occasional disturbances at labour exchanges, or government offices, and clashes with the police. And in August 1959 there were severe riots involving North African Jews in the Wadi Salib quarter of

114

Haifa; seven people were injured, and seventy were arrested before order was restored.

Another cause of consternation to the government was the growing sense of isolation of a large part of Israel from the Jewish world outside it, and even a wish to dissociate itself from the whole Jewish past.

In 1960 some 40 per cent of the population of Israel was native-born, and a good proportion of it felt no particular sense of identity with the Jewish communities outside. A course of study on diaspora Jewry was established in the state schools, but in May 1960 a more dramatic opportunity to acquaint the young people of Israel with the immediate Jewish past, and possibly to draw all sections of Israel together into a common sense of identity with Jews outside, presented itself. Adolf Eichmann had been arrested.

The Eichmann trial, though it brought an arch-enemy of Jewry to justice, did not have quite the effect which Ben Gurion had hoped for. A generation of young people brought up to fight for their every right, self-confident, assertive, almost aggressive, could not understand how European Jews could have gone so meekly to their slaughter, and if anything the trial may have widened the distance between young Israel and the diaspora.

In June 1958 the cabinet was shaken by another religious crisis.

The religious parties – there are, as we have seen, four of them grouped into two pairs – are less rigid in their views on foreign or economic issues than on religious issues and Ben Gurion, therefore, found them on the whole less awkward partners in his coalitions than either Mapam on the left, or the General Zionists on the right, especially as, while by no means religious himself, he admired many of the traditions and values preserved by the religious groups. Thus, he had been content to leave such matters as marriage and divorce in the hands of the ecclesiastical authorities (where they had been placed by the British administration), nor was he seriously opposed to the demands of his religious partners for stricter Sabbatarian laws. On occasion, however, he felt that they had over-reached themselves, and this happened in 1958.

The issue was Who is a Jew? The question is less simple than it seems. In Jewish law a person is a Jew if he is the child of a Jewish mother or has been converted by a recognized Rabbinical court. The Minister of the Interior, Israel Bar-Yehuda (Ahdut Avoda) had ruled that 'Jewish nationality' could for purposes of registration be applied to anyone who declared he was a Jew and did not profess any other faith, or was the child of parents who declared themselves to be Jewish.

Dr Zerach Warhaftig (who was then Deputy Minister of Religion) protested that this was a 'fateful decision likely to destroy the Jewish people', and he and four other government colleagues, Moshe Shapiro (Minister of Social Welfare and Religion), Dr Josef Burg (Minister of Posts), Moshe Unna (Deputy Minister of Education) and Rabbi Israel Rosenberg (Deputy Minister of Social Welfare) resigned. The government, however, had a majority without the religious parties, and was able to continue in office.

In the following year, however, there came another crisis, stemming this time from the left.

In June 1959 strong feelings were aroused by reports that Israel had agreed to supply West Germany with 250,000 grenade throwers. In a heated Knesset debate on the government's action, two Ahdut Avoda Ministers (Israel Bar-Yehuda and Moshe Carmel) and two Mapam Ministers (Israel Barzilai and Mordecai Ben Tov) voted against it. Ben Gurion thereupon demanded their resignations. When they refused, he resigned, protesting that he could not head a government where the principle of collective responsibility was not recognized. He was eventually persuaded to return to office, and agreed to do so on a caretaker basis.

In November 1959 the life of the Knesset ended and new elections were held. There were few surprises. The electorate had grown by about 100,000 since 1955. There had been the triumph of Sinai, and comparative prosperity, but there were few important shifts. Mapai made some gains at the expense of Ahdut Avoda and the General Zionists. Herut improved its position a little, probably at the expense of the General Zionists. Some Arab grievances had been rectified, and this no doubt affected the communists, who lost

3 seats. But Mapai, with 47 seats, was well short of the 61 it needed for an overall majority. Ben Gurion spoke of the need for a different electoral system, based on the British model of the single member constituency. In the meantime he had to content himself with the same coalition as before, that is, Mapai, Mapam, Ahdut Avoda, the National Religious Party, and the Progressives.

The elections brought into the Knesset a number of new figures, including Abba Eban, Moshe Dayan and Shimon Peres, all on the Mapai list. Eban had served Israel with distinction as Ambassador to the United States and Permanent Representative at the United Nations, especially during and after the Sinai campaign; Dayan was the victor of Sinai, and Peres, as Director General of the Ministry of Defence, had been one of the main organizers of the victory. All three received office, Eban as Minister of Education, Peres as Ben Gurion's right-hand man in Defence, and Dayan as Minister of Agriculture.

The political life of the country, that is, the ruling circles of Mapai and the Histadrut, were still dominated by Ben Gurion and his contemporaries who arrived from Russia during the Second Aliya or a little later, and after Sinai there was a feeling that they had been clinging to office a little too long. The bestowal of office on Eban, Peres and Dayan was in part an attempt to meet this criticism.

The 'young ones', as they were called, were not so very young. Peres was 36 but Eban and Dayan were 44.

The life of the 1959 Knesset was nasty, brutal and short, and it was the Prime Minister himself who cut it short. The cause was the Lavon affair.

In the autumn of 1954 a security operation by Israel agents in Egypt ended in disaster. The ring-leaders were arrested and hanged. Lavon, who was Minister of Defence at the time, claimed that the order for the operation had been given by a senior officer without his knowledge; the senior officer protested that he had acted on the orders of Lavon. At the latter's request Sharett, who was then Prime Minister, ordered an inquiry which, however, failed to establish the facts of the case and Lavon resigned and moved side-ways to become Secretray General of the Histadrut. That was not the end of the issue. Further investigations followed, culminating finally in an inquiry by a cabinet committee which found that Lavon had *not* given the order which had led to the Cairo disaster. Ben Gurion, however, would not accept these findings, which he called a miscarriage of justice, and in January 1961 he resigned.

Attempts to form a government without him failed and in March the Knesset dissolved itself.

In April, with the active encouragement of Dr Nahum Gold-mann, President of the World Zionist Organization, the General Zionists and the Progressives came together under the leadership of Dr Pinhas Rosen, Minister of Justice in the outgoing government, to form the Liberal Party. They had 14 seats between them in the fourth Knesset and as such did not yet represent a challenge to the left-wing parties, but they did introduce an unpredictable element in the all too predictable party line-up, and the results of the election were awaited with great interest. But again there were no fundamental changes. Mapai won 42 seats, 5 down from its all-time peak in 1959, but still on top. Herut came second again, and again with 17 seats. The Liberals came third with 17, a gain of 3. The National Religious Party kept the 12 seats it had won in the previous election, and Mapam its 9. Ahdut Avoda recovered one of the 3 seats it lost in 1959 and now had 8.

Ben Gurion returned to office, but not for long.

Public opinion in Israel is always volatile on anything involving Germany, and fierce indignation was caused by reports early in 1963 that German scientists were engaged on war-work in Egypt.

Ever since the signing of the Reparations Agreement, the cul-tivation of a productive relationship with Western Germany had been one of the cornerstones of Ben Gurion's foreign policy. He defended that policy when he was attacked for trying to procure German arms, and defended it again over the sale of arms to Ger-many, and he did not wish to embarrass the Federal Republic unduly by exaggerating the number and value of German scientists working in Egypt. Mrs Golda Meir, his Foreign Minister, did not share this view, and neither did the Knesset. In March it passed a resolution calling on the Federal Government to end the activities of German

118

scientists engaged in the Egyptian war effort. Three months later Ben Gurion resigned. His resignation, he said, had nothing to do with affairs of state, but was due to 'purely personal reasons'.

He was succeeded by his Finance Minister, Levi Eshkol.

Eshkol was one of those who had come from Russia with the Second Aliya. He was born in 1895, settled in Palestine at the age of 18 and served in the Jewish Legion in the First World War. He was a founder of Kibbutz Degania Bet and Kiryat Anavim but became more and more involved in administration and was eventually swallowed up by the Histadrut machine and rose to become Secretary General. During the War of Liberation he was Director-General of the Ministry of Defence. In 1950 he became Treasurer of the Jewish Agency. In the following year he was elected to the Second Knesset and was appointed Minister of Agriculture. In 1952, on the death of Eliezer Kaplan, he was appointed to what was perhaps the most impossible office in the state, the Ministry of Finance.

Eshkol has none of the dynamism, colour or zeal of Ben Gurion – and the country was probably glad of it. It wanted a rest from the successive jolts administered by 'The Old Man', as Ben Gurion is popularly known, and to enjoy its passing prosperity in peace.

If Ben Gurion was the Winston Churchill of Israel, Eshkol is perhaps the Attlee, only without the same capacity of making decisions and sticking to them. He is a patient slogger, a capable administrator, a good machine man, and in many ways typical of the solid Commissars who rule Mapai, the Histadrut, the country.

But he was hardly settled in office, when the whole foundation of the Mapai-Histadrut establishment was shaken by its principal creator – Ben Gurion. There were two causes. The first was the second phase of the Lavon affair; the second was Ben Gurion's determination to reform the country's electoral system.

Ben Gurion, when he walked out of the premiership over the Lavon affair in 1961, had not been content to let the matter rest. He dislodged Lavon from his office as Secretary General of the Histadrut, and he instituted his own inquiry which satisfied him, at least, that Lavon *had* given the fatal order which led to the 1954 security disaster. Eshkol, however, with the backing of the Mapai secretariat, did not propose to take the matter further.

At the same time talks were going on for an alignment between Mapai and Ahdut Avoda. This was a perfectly natural development. Once the latter had broken from Mapam, the former was its natural partner. It had been more determinedly socialist than Mapai, but that was ebbing. It had been more nationalistic, but that, in the comparative tranquillity of the early sixties, was a diminishing force. It was, however, strongly opposed to electoral reform. Eshkol was willing to compromise on this issue. Ben Gurion, who looked on electoral reform as a panacea for Israel's political ills, was not.

He was joined in his opposition to Eshkol by two of the 'young ones', Moshe Dayan and Shimon Peres, by Yosef Almogy, Minister of Development, and several other Mapai members of the Knesset. Dayan had been Chief of Staff at the time of the 1954 security disaster, and Peres Director-General of the Ministry of Defence, and both, apart from personal loyalty to Ben Gurion, believed that they had good cause to support his stand on the Lavon affair.

But there was more involved than either the affair or electoral reform. There was the feeling that the old guard in Mapai and the Histadrut were ossified in their attitudes and incapable of ruling post-Sinai Israel.

When the Mapai secretariat backed Eshkol both on Lavon and his alignment policy, Ben Gurion and his associates formed a new party, the Reshimat Poalei Yisrael (the Israel Workers' List) or Rafi. Electoral reform was placed at the head of its programme, and it undertook 'to correct a situation where the country is in the hands of a generation of old-timers that travels in limousines yet thinks in terms of living in tents', and 'to rectify a situation where the individual citizen is lost in the face of proliferating bureaucracies whether of the government, Jewish Agency or Histadrut'.[55]

While Mapai was falling apart, the parties on the right were drawing together. The Liberal Party which had been formed by the fusion of the General Zionists and Progressives in 1961 voted in April 1965 to form a joint parliamentary and electoral list with Herut. The confusion on the left gave the right a hope of offering an alternative to the inevitable Mapai-led coalition, provided it could present a united front. The union, however, was incomplete because 7 of the 17 Knesset members, representing almost the whole of the Progressive wing, including Pinhas Rosen, refused to join. Herut was too militantly right wing for their tastes. The union became known as Gahal; the dissenters called themselves the Independent Liberals.

The split in Mapai worried many observers that no party might emerge from the forthcoming elections with a large enough nucleus to form a government, and that democracy might be imperilled.

They need not have worried.

The Mapai-Ahdut Avoda alignment won 45 seats, 5 less than in the previous election, which they had fought separately. But 45 seats for a party which had lost its leader, and had not emerged fully from its civil war, was an excellent result. It demonstrated also the almost invincible power of the Mapai machine. Rafi won 10 seats. Gahal's bid for power was abortive. It had 27 members in the old Knesset, it now had 26, and the Independent Liberals lost 2 seats and were reduced to 5. The NRP lost a seat, and Mapam lost 1. There had also been a split in the Communist party, between the pro-Peking wing, which was mostly Arab, and the Moscow wing, which was still substantially Jewish. The former kept the 3 seats it had in the old Knesset, the latter lost 1 of its 2 seats.

And for the first time an Independent member was elected.

The country had hardly rested from the elections before Ben Gurion began agitating anew for electoral reform.

Israel's electoral system has the virtue of being democratic. If a party gets, say, 10 per cent of the votes it will get 10 per cent of the seats. The lottery element, which one finds in the British system, is removed. It has the serious disadvantage that as the whole country is treated as one constituency, and the electoral hopes of a candidate rest entirely on his position in the party list, too much power is left with the parties. This is also the case in the municipal elections. The cities are not divided into wards but each party presents its own list, and the elector votes not for an individual but a symbol. The best that an individual can do is to present himself as a party. This was in fact done by Mr Uri Avenari in the 1965 election and he was returned. But Mr Avenari is the proprietor of Israel's most popular magazine, a scandal sheet called *Ha'olam Hazeh*, which helped him win his seat. Others have tried it and failed.

The effect of the system is to limit political independence and put a premium on conformity. One becomes the servant of the party secretariat rather than the constituent. The constituent – and this is the most serious defect of the system – is not in touch with his own particular member to whom he can bring a complaint, and it is sometimes difficult to get a grievance aired in Israel without staging a riot.

Ben Gurion also feels that the Israeli system leads to the proliferation of parties, and hence political instability, and he would like to see it replaced by the British system.

Israel politics are, in fact, not all that unstable. Israel has had six General Elections since 1949, and so has Britain. Moreover, the parties have been drawing together, and every succeeding election has seen a fall in their numbers. The existence of the religious question, which in its way is peculiar to Israel, has prevented the emergence of an effective right-wing party, and therefore an alternative ruling group. In a constituency system the Mizrachi, at least, would probably be forced to go into a huddle with the Liberals and Herut, but that is by no means certain.

What must also have made Ben Gurion impatient with the present system is that the Prime Minister is unable to form the team he wants, but is involved in a system of horse-trading with the different parties as to who should have what. Colleagues are imposed upon him rather than chosen by him.

Finally the fact that every government has been a coalition has meant that even urgent policies are constantly whittled down by compromise, or that in order to gain agreement on one issue concessions have had to be made on quite another. The energies of the cabinet are spent on bargaining rather than ruling.

9   Six days that shook the earth

IN THE SPRING OF 1967 the main concern of Israel was economic. The balance of trade had improved a little, but there was a depression and its effects were becoming widespread. Half-completed blocks of flats stood amidst sand and gravel, abandoned by contractors who could not pay their men. In the early mornings men and boys jostled at the labour exchanges for available jobs. The citrus season was drawing to a close and soon the number of unemployed— already approaching the 100,000 mark—would be swollen. The rate of immigration had declined to a trickle; the rate of emigration was rising, and among the emigrants were people with the highest professional qualifications.

In March it was learned that two employees of the scandal sheet *Bul* had been imprisoned for publishing an article linking Israel's security services with the Ben Barka affair. What scandalized the public was not the allegations in the article, which were almost certainly untrue, but the fact that the men were arrested in secret, tried in secret, and imprisoned in secret. Israel got to hear of it only through a leak in the *New York Times*.

When the *Jewish Observer*, the organ of the British Zionist Federation, called for the resignation of Moshe Shapiro, the Minister of Justice, there were protests from Mr Levi Eshkol, the Prime Minister. When the *Jewish Observer* went on to describe the economic scene in Israel in its full, sombre colours, the editor was dismissed.

Mr Eshkol's office intervened when a students' magazine at the Hebrew University carried a cartoon on the *Bul* affair. There was, Mr Eshkol said later, something deficient in the patriotism of Jewish students and he urged teachers at the Hebrew University to instil a deeper love of the land.

Friends of Israel were becoming worried about the mood of the country.

The Sinai campaign of 1956 had brought peace to the southern frontiers. A United Nations Emergency Force was stationed in Sinai and the Gaza strip. Border settlements were able to go about their work without harassment from marauders and Israeli ships passed back and forth through the Straits of Tiran without let or hindrance.

In the north the situation was otherwise. Successive régimes in Damascus vied with each other in their militancy. There were frequent rumblings on the Syrian frontier and these grew in volume. There was shelling from the Syrian heights above the Sea of Galilee and incursions from marauders operating on much the same principles as the Egyptian *Fedayeen*. They called themselves *El Fatah*. They were based in Syria and trained there, but they generally operated from Jordanian or Lebanese territory. In 1965 *El Fatah* carried out thirty-five terrorist raids.

The Syrian government openly affirmed its support for the terrorists and in a broadcast on 11 October 1966 the Syrian Prime Minister declared: 'We are not protectors of Israel security. We shall never restrain the revolution of Palestinian people who are seeking to liberate their homeland.'

In 1966, terrorists made 41 incursions into Israel killing 10 people and injuring 36. It is not difficult to imagine how Ben Gurion would have reacted in such a situation. Mr Eshkol took the matter to the Security Council, but a resolution calling upon Syria to strengthen measures against infiltration was vetoed by the USSR on 4 November. On 13 November units of the Israeli army, including tanks and artillery, launched a fierce attack on the village of Samu – in Jordan – resulting in serious loss of life and destruction of property.

There was widespread criticism of the action both inside and outside Israel. The government's case was that Jordan had not done enough to check the passage of terrorists through its territory and that Samu in particular had been a terrorist base.

On 7 April 1967, after prolonged shelling of kibbutzim near the Sea of Galilee, Israel sent up aircraft to silence the Syrian battery. An air-battle ensued in which the Syrians lost six Russian-built jets.

The incident did not bring peace to the border. Terrorist incidents multiplied. On 14 May, Israel Independence Day, Mr Eshkol warned that a confrontation with Syria was inevitable if the attacks continued. It cannot be said with any degree of certainty whether the government actually planned to invade Syria, or even launch a heavy reprisal attack, though it would have been perfectly within its rights had it done so. Every other means had been tried to bring peace to its border, but without success.

In November 1966 a defence pact had been signed between Syria and Egypt. It was not brought into operation during the air-battle on 7 April, but on 16 May Egypt declared a state of emergency. Two days later President Nasser asked the United Nations to withdraw its Emergency Force from Sinai and Gaza, and U Thant at once complied.

In Cairo the Minister of Religion called on religious leaders to declare a *Jihad* against Israel to regain Palestine for the Arabs. On 21 May there was full mobilization in Egypt and Israel, and in Damascus the Minister of Defence, Hafez el Assad, declared that his army was ready 'not only to repel Israeli aggression but to take the initiative in liberating Palestine and destroying the Zionist presence in the Arab homeland'.

On 23 May Egypt closed the Straits of Tiran to Israel-bound shipping. 'We know the closing of the Gulf of Aqaba might mean war with Israel', President Nasser told a gathering of Arab trade unionists.

On 25 May Israel's Foreign Minister, Abba Eban, embarked on a tour of Paris, London and Washington to see what help Israel could expect from the Western powers. France, which had shown the warmest sympathy for Israel, and which had supplied her air force (at a price), now kept herself coldly aloof, almost hostile. The United States and Britain counselled patience and spoke vaguely of a league of maritime nations securing free passage of the Straits of Tiran. The United States further undertook to make good the economic losses resulting from the blockade. Israel was thrown back on to herself.

By the end of May Israel had been under arms for a week. Her army of 70,000 had grown to 230,000. Streets emptied as vehicles and their owners were mobilized. Schools closed. Some factories had to shut down for lack of manpower. School-children took over the sorting and delivery of mail and the collection of refuse. Hotels were requisitioned for use as emergency hospitals.

The politicians, as we shall see, still found time and energy for some in-fighting, but over the country as a whole the grumbling, the cynicism, the divisions had all but ceased. The religious groups who had been organizing demonstrations and daubing walls in a cam-paign to make autopsies illegal, began to organize prayer meetings. The Sabbath laws were suspended and Jews in side-curls rushed to bear arms. No one doubted what the consequences of defeat would be. The prospect of death concentrates a nation's unity marvellously. Israel was a coiled spring bent for action. But as yet there was only talk.

The army was confident, even cocky, that if it came to war it would not lose, but there was a crisis of confidence in the civilian leadership. Mr Eshkol, whatever his qualities, and they are many, is not a forceful man of action. His genius for compromise, which was not always appreciated in times of peace, was of little value in dealing with Nasser, for Nasser had left no room for compromise. At a similar pass in Britain's fortunes the House of Commons turned against Chamberlain and brought in Churchill. In Israel the Knesset has no such power, and the issue was settled at the head office of Mapai, by the party secretariat.

Mr Eshkol was both Prime Minister and Minister of Defence, and pressure began to build up in the country as well as the cabinet for the appointment of a military figure to the latter office. There was one such figure already in the cabinet, Yigal Allon, the Minister of Labour, who had commanded the victorious troops on the southern front during the War of Liberation. He was not a member of the ruling Mapai but in the Ahdut Avoda, with whom Mapai had formed a united front in the 1964 elections. When Mr Eshkol saw the extent of feeling against him, he was prepared to hand over to Allon, but by then it was too late, for the demand had grown for a government of national unity embracing all the parties except the communists, and for Moshe Dayan to be Defence Minister in that government.

Mr Eshkol still hesitated and was supported by Mrs Golda Meir, Secretary General of Mapai. Dayan, it must be remembered, was not only outside Mapai, but he was a member of the Rafi party which had broken away from Mapai. The majority of the party secretariat, however, felt that this was no time for such considera-tions. Mr Eshkol and Mrs Meir were outvoted. On 1 June the government was widened. Mr Menahem Beigin of Gahal, the former head of Irgun Tzvai Leumi, who had been kept out of all previous governments by Ben Gurion, and Mr Joseph Sapir, of the Liberal Party, were brought in as Ministers Without Portfolio. Moshe Dayan was made Minister of Defence.

To the beleaguered Israeli public this was almost an omen of victory in itself. People cheered the news and embraced each other in the streets.

For weeks the air of the Middle East had been filled with threats of extermination. Mr Ahmed Shukeiry, head of the Palestine Liberation Army, asked what would happen to the Jews in the event of an Arab victory, said that only Jews born in Palestine would be allowed to remain, 'but I think none of them will be left alive'.

Syria and Egypt already had a defence pact and as the threat of war became more acute other Arab states, including Morocco, Algeria, Tunisia, Libya, Lebanon, Iraq, Saudi Arabia, Sudan and Kuwait, gave promises of men and money. It was a familiar roll-call which did not unduly worry Israel but when Hussein flew to Cairo for his dramatic meeting with Nasser, there was undisguised consternation. Jordan overlooked the Tel-Aviv–Jerusalem highway and it was within shelling distance of Tel-Aviv itself. It could, by thrusting ten miles towards the sea at Hadera, cut Israel in half. And there was a healthy respect for the fighting spirit of the Jordanian army. The appointment of Dayan was thus a necessary morale booster.

To the man in the street the very name of Dayan meant victory, much as the name Eshkol meant indecision; but it is unlikely that without him in the cabinet the war would have been delayed by a day, or that it would have taken a different course.

On 5 June the fighting began. There was some speculation in the British press as to who fired the first shot. The question is not particularly relevant. Israel and the Arab states were in a state of war, and had been so since 1948. Arab leaders had made this clear on innumerable occasions. That was Egypt's excuse for keeping the Suez Canal closed to Israeli shipping, and, latterly, for the closing of the Straits of Tiran. It was the excuse for the economic blockade of Israel which had been rigorously maintained since 1948. President Nasser had frequently declared his intention to liquidate the Jewish state at the opportune moment, and it now seemed that he thought the moment was opportune. Arab rivalries had been patched up. Nasser had poured a vast army into Sinai, and a large, Soviet-equipped air force was poised to attack Israel's highly concentrated centres of population on the sea coast. He had rockets. He had used gas in the Yemen, and Israel hastily acquired gas masks from West Germany. Jordan was ready with her army in the centre, and Syria on the north; Iraq had sent one contingent into Sinai and another into Jordan. Algeria too was sending troops.

Israel by her very claim to existence could not have allowed Egypt to blockade her sea-roads, or Syria to continue harassing her settlements. It was equally clear that the United Nations was useless in this situation, and that the great powers either would or could do nothing to change it. Mr Eshkol had warned Egypt that the blockade of the Straits of Tiran would mean war and President Nasser, although he had achieved a great deal by bluff, could hardly have hoped to avoid war now. He had made war inevitable, and once it was inevitable it would have been criminal for the Israeli government to let the Arabs choose the most convenient moment to attack. If Israel was to win, the war had to be swift, sharp and decisive. In the event it was settled on the first day, even in the first hours.

At 7 a.m. of 5 June Israeli planes attacked Arab air bases in Egypt, Syria, Jordan and Iraq, and destroyed over 400 planes on the ground. Jordan's small air force of 16 Hawker-Hunter jets was completely wiped out. There were fierce tank battles in Sinai and in the Gaza strip. At 11 a.m. Jordan opened a second front against Israel. There was shelling of the New City of Jerusalem and hand-to-hand fighting in the Old. By the end of the first day Israel had thrust forward to the sea at the base of the Gaza strip and had cut off Shukeiry's Palestine Liberation Army. On the second day Gaza fell and the Israelis advanced to El Arish, forty miles inside Sinai. On the third day they took Sharm el-Sheik, near the tip of the Sinai peninsula, overlooking the Straits of Tiran – the immediate source of the whole conflict.

In Jerusalem Israel could not make use of her absolute mastery of the air for fear of damaging the holy places, and the use of artillery and mortars had to be restricted. The advance was therefore slow and bloody, but by the end of the third day the Old City had fallen. Jerusalem was reunited and after nearly 2,000 years the Jews were once again in full control of the City of David. Nablus and Jericho had been taken a little earlier, as well as the towns of Jenin, Hebron and Bethlehem, and the entire west bank of the Kingdom of Jordan was in Jewish hands. An emergency meeting of the Security Council called for a cease-fire, and on 7 June King Hussein, with his army shattered and air force destroyed, accepted. The Egyptians, in full retreat across Sinai, held out for two days longer.

In the north the Syrians issued daily communiques of victories over the Israeli forces, of advances on Nazareth and Safad, but sat tight behind their fortifications. Israel now turned upon them, advanced to Kuneitra, about half-way between the border and Damascus, and then fanned out eastwards to take the ridges over-looking Galilee. By Sunday, 11 June, the fighting was over. 'It was', wrote James Cameron, 'probably the most sensationally swift, surgical, complete and pitiless campaign in the records of war.'

The fourteenth of June was the Feast of Pentecost, when Jews celebrate the anniversary of the granting of the law of Moses on Mt Sinai. It was traditional in ancient times for them to go up to Jerusalem to commemorate the occasion in the courtyard of the Temple. The second Temple was destroyed in AD 70, and only the 'Wailing Wall' – closed to Jews since 1948 – remained. It was now open again, and on 14 June 200,000 Jews surged to the wall to watch, to pray, to exult. The 'Wailing Wall' had become the Wall of Triumph.

10　　The land and the people

ISRAEL HAS NEARLY QUADRUPLED her population in the past eighteen years, and bears every sign of it – homes quickly erected, their bottom stories in use before the top ones are complete; suburbs thrown together before there are roads to serve them; whole towns imposed upon inhospitable sands.

There is Arad. Like most places in Israel it has its Biblical connections: 'And the Canaanite, the king of Arad, who dwelt in the south, heard tell that Israel came . . . and he fought against Israel and took some of them captive.'[56] It had no other claim to fame, and until recently it was a white, rockstrewn ridge, some 2,000 ft high, facing the Wilderness of Judea to the north, and the Dead Sea to the east. Today it is a town of some 2,000 souls, loud with children and the rattle of concrete mixers.

By Israeli standards it is in the middle of nowhere. Thirty miles separate it from Beersheba, the capital of the Negev and nearest sizeable town, and as one climbs towards it past bedouin encampments and scrub land, it begins to loom somewhat improbably out of the surrounding sands. The tall buildings quiver in the heat and it does not quite look as if it has a right to be there.

It was founded in 1961 after natural gas had been struck at nearby Rosh Zohar. The gas reserves were not as large as was originally hoped and Arad has not grown as rapidly as was originally planned, but it is there, solid, the streets busy, the blocks of flats rising like ramparts on every side.

The elevated position of Arad, which gives it some relief from the heat of summer, leaves it exposed to the winds of winter, and it is blasted at times by raging sandstorms, but the air is usually dry, and it is one of the more salubrious points in the Negev. Travellers pause there en route to Masada or the Dead Sea. There is an hotel, a restaurant, even an art gallery, and a colonnade of shops flanking one side of a small square.

This is the town centre and in the mornings it is thronged with young housewives in stretch slacks and bulging blouses, their hair clipped Bond Street fashion. Most young housewives in Israel go out to work. In Arad they have fewer employment opportunities, and less need to seek employment. Wages are high, tax incentives are generous, and rents are low. Most of the men are employed in the Dead Sea potash works, some twenty miles downhill in the Arava, and they commute daily. It is a compact community, youthful, hardy and, by Israeli standards, homogeneous.

Dimona, twenty miles across the hills to the south, as the crow flies, and fifty by road, is another new town, much larger than Arad and a good deal more heterogeneous. A considerable number of its wage earners are also employed in the Dead Sea works, but it has a large textile plant, numerous small enterprises and, a few miles across the grey sands to the south, the immense gleaming sphere of Israel's nuclear energy reactor.

Founded in 1955 Dimona has a population of some 18,000, made up largely of immigrants from India and Morocco. It is already large enough to have different quarters, those occupied by the professional and managerial class employed at the reactor or in the factories, and those occupied by factory hands; and old enough to show signs of decay. It is in fact a town like many others in Israel, the houses rectangular boxes three stories high, fronted by balconies festooned with washing; the shops sheltered behind colonnades; the town square a plaza on Italian lines, but dominated by a cinema instead of a cathedral.

One gets an exaggerated idea of distance in Israel. It is a small country and covers an area of only 8,000 square miles, or 77 per cent of mandated Palestine. Its entire length of 280 miles could be traversed in seven or eight hours, but within its confines one can meet considerable variations in climate and fantastic variations in scene. At Ashkelon, on the Mediterranean shore near the Egyptian border, one is among red sands, waving palm trees, and squat, glossy orange trees, sagging with fruit. The heat is always tolerable and often pleasant, and on a spring day people wear sweaters to keep warm. There are red-roofed villas in the sands, green lawns, gardens. Yet an hour's drive to the south, beyond Dimona, brings one upon a lunar landscape of bare rock, of chasms and canyons, and a heat that sits on one like lead. Galilee in the north can get nearly 1,000 mm. of rainfall a year, and the southern Mediterranean shore about 500, but beyond Beersheba there is little or no rainfall. Sodom gets about 50 mm. a year, Eilat about 20. There is hardly any vegetation beyond the thorny scrub growing along the sides of dry, rock-strewn gullies. Sometimes a blistering east wind— the *khamsin* — can blow for days on end, dry and intense as the blast of a furnace, making it difficult to work by day or sleep by night. And when the *khamsin* stops the sandstorms can start.

Before 1948 the whole area now known as the Negev was largely uninhabited, but it could not be allowed to remain so for it covers some 4,716 square miles, or more than half of the land area of the whole Jewish state. As Ben Gurion never tired of asserting, the future of Israel lay in the Negev.

In 1943 the Jewish Agency had set up three research stations in the area at Gevulot, Revivim and Beit Eshel, and found that large parts of the Negev could be cultivated, given sufficient water. The soil itself was fundamentally fertile. Since then water has been brought to the western Negev, first by small bore pipe-line, and more recently by the national carrier.

It has proved somewhat more difficult to bring people south, but slowly and persistently, in a joint effort between the government and the Jewish Agency, a thick cluster of settlements has been established among the sands flanking the Egyptian-held Gaza strip.

Most of the settlers in the south are Sephardim, for immigrants from African and Asian countries can adapt themselves more easily to the torrid temperatures of the region. There was also the

133

more relevant fact that fewer of them had the hope of securing a foothold in the north.

Immigrants are not directed as such to any particular area. If they have relatives, contacts, a profession, vendable skills, they go wherever they choose. If they are dependent wholly on the Jewish Agency they are directed to where they can be most usefully employed, and as the north has been thoroughly exploited they have generally been sent south, to be settled on the land.

There have been disappointments. Omer, for example, is today being developed as a suburb of Beersheba. It had been planned as a moshav for Indian immigrants, but they failed to take root, abandoned homes and lands, and drifted into the towns.

Overall, however, the results have been amazing. Inveterate townsmen without agricultural experience or skill have, with a little guidance and a great deal of perseverance, been able to wrest an enviable living from a reluctant soil. Settlers who began life in one bare room and with a small patch of land as recently as ten years ago, live in comfortable, well-furnished dwellings, and have become part of Israel's class of yeoman farmers formed by the older moshavim.

In the uplands towards Eilat neither toil nor water can make anything grow, and the small towns scattered about the area live largely on mining and quarrying, and selling drinks to passing tourists. And they pass in their tens of thousands – school-children by the lorry-load, brought from the north to see the south, singing along the way in sun-parched voices; travellers from abroad in air-conditioned buses, or packed tight, shoulder to shoulder, in long, black taxis, darting upwards and downwards round the mountain passes, or panting slowly behind massive Autocar tractors piled high with potash, wending their way towards the rail-head near Beersheba.

Beersheba itself has undergone a change in size and a metamorphosis in character. A little more than a decade ago it had the self-conscious air of a frontier town. Men came wheeling in from outlying settlements on bicycles, or in jeeps, with rifles on their back. It was hardly more than one long dusty street, with the desert thrusting in among the flag-stones. One felt on the edge of nowhere.

It is now a city with inner suburbs and outer suburbs, restaurants with Diners' Club signs, discothèques. The main hotels have camels tethered in their courtyards, and there are bedouins in the street, but there is no mistaking its direction as a minor Tel-Aviv.

This is a fate which is threatening other growing towns, for it is difficult in a country so small to escape the influence of a city so large and multifarious.

Tel-Aviv has a population of 400,000, but it is part of an almost continuous urban sprawl stretching from Holon in the south to Herzliya in the north and which, including Bat Yam, Givatayim, Ramat Gan, Benei Beraq, Petach Tikva and Ramat Hasharon, contains about half of the population of the country.

Tel-Aviv is the metropolis of Israel. It is the commercial centre, the arts centre, the centre of communications. Although the seat of government is formally in Jerusalem many of the government offices are still in Tel-Aviv, and so are the embassies of those states which have not yet recognized Jerusalem as the capital. The political parties as well as the Histadrut have their head offices in Tel-Aviv, and Tel-Aviv is the home of all the national papers of Israel save the *Jerusalem Post*.

It is a thoroughly utilitarian, functional, hard-headed this-worldly. city, dusty, hot, humid, sweating, but tireless.

It operates in top gear with results that are not often com-mensurate with the speed or the effort, as if pace was almost a quality in itself.

The working day begins early and during the long break for lunch, while the middle-aged turn in for their *siestas* (one somehow does not see many *old* people in Tel-Aviv – especially when com-pared to Jerusalem, which is almost a gerontopolis), the young, in the briefest of briefs and mini bikinis, descend upon the shore in their tens of thousands till one cannot see sands for people. And at night, they move north towards Dizengoff square, with its cafés, cinemas, discotheques, and the square itself with its broad walks and its fountains. To be there is an evening out in its own right, and the square has given a new word to the Hebrew language, *Le-hizdangev*, to promenade, to see and be seen.

It is nearly midnight before the crowds begin to thin, but many of the cafés remain open, with earnest voices arguing over coffee till the small hours of the morning.

Jerusalem, with its 188,000 people, is by comparison provincial, and has about it something of the air of an English cathedral town.

It is a university city, a city of synagogues and *yeshivot*, churches, monasteries and convents, white domes, turrets, towers, against a clear, blue sky. There life is more casual and a good deal less worldly. Tel-Aviv is in an eternal hurry. Jerusalem is content to let the world go by.

There is one part of the town, Mea Shearim, which has almost written off this world. A large notice greets one at the entrance in three languages: 'O Daughter of Israel. The Torah obliges you to dress with modesty. We do not tolerate people passing through our streets immodestly dressed. Committee for Guarding Modesty.'

Mea Shearim is an area of narrow, winding streets, with small stone houses with wrought-iron verandas and sagging shutters, and it is one of the capital's favourite tourist attractions, not only because it is out of this world, but because it preserves something of the world from which much of Israel, and many tourists, stem.

Jerusalem is perched high on the Judean hills, and is cooler in summer than the coastal plain below. It can be cold in winter, and it has experienced the occasional blizzard. Its air for much of the year is invigorating, but even in the depth of summer, when the very buildings seem to sag with heat, there are evening breezes which restore it to life.

It is, unlike Tel-Aviv, a city of infinite variety, with unexpected courtyards and gardens at the end of narrow streets, and different vistas at every turn. During the Mandate all new building had to be of local stone, which is a creamy white, or pink, in colour. This ordinance has not been fully maintained, but local stone continues to be used at least for the façades of new buildings, and the city continues to charm.

But nothing becomes new Jerusalem so much as the prospect of the old, the Tower of David, the city wall standing on Crusader foundations, the towers and minarets peering above it.

If one approaches Jerusalem from Tel-Aviv by train one passes through Arab villages with women working in the field, reaping corn, or gathering it with their hands, like a Bible illustration come to life.

One sometimes deplores the very thing one most admires about Israel, the pace of change. In Jerusalem one is less conscious of it.

In Haifa, however, one gets back to the pace of Tel-Aviv. It is a city of over 200,000 people, ever growing, ever changing. It has wound its way up Mount Carmel till it has toppled over the crest and is now making its way down over the other side. And it is growing northwards in an ever-extending industrial zone, past the oil refinery, along Haifa Bay towards Acre, and southwards, along the coastal plain, towards Athlit.

Tel-Aviv is about an hour's journey to the south, and one passes few stretches of land unbroken by habitations. One can see the two sprawls meeting within the next decade.

There is intense rivalry between the two cities, and as Tel-Aviv has recently acquired a university, Haifa, which already has a humanities faculty within its splendid Technion, and a small University, is to have a large one, a vast monolith designed by Oscar Niemeyer.

Tel-Aviv is more inward looking. It lies at the heart of the country and is far more Israel than, say, Paris is France. Haifa is more outward looking. Its situation high on the hill, overlooking the port and the bay, with the ships in dock, or at anchor, would in itself assure this. But it is more self-consciously European. One hears more German than one hears in any large town in Israel. It is wealthy because of its port and industries, and also because a great many people with money have chosen to live there. It is as energetic as Tel-Aviv, but exudes less sweat.

Moving north-west from Haifa one ascends the hills of Galilee, rounded and boulder-strewn, and crowned at various points by kibbutzim and moshavim. Near Safad one comes upon Mt Meron (3,692 ft), the highest point in the country.

Safad, once the city of the mystics, and still with its small group of scholars bent over the *Kabala*, is, because of its high altitude, a much-favoured summer resort. It has a summer temperature which hovers in the seventies, while Tiberias, some 20 miles below, on the Sea of Galilee (and 665 ft below sea-level), lies sweltering in the nineties.

Tiberias, however, has the advantage in the winter and it used to be said that the inhabitants of Safad go to Tiberias in the winter, and those of Tiberias to Safad in the summer.

Beyond the Sea of Galilee, in the very north, like a green finger poking into Syria, is the Hula valley. To the south, between the Hills of Gilboa and the River Jordan is the Beth Shan valley.

Both the Hula area and the Beth Shan valley are extremely fertile, with black, rich soil and abundant water. And north-eastwards from Beth Shan, towards Haifa, is the Valley of Jezreel.

One can see the entire valley, which is about thirty miles long, at a glance from Tivon, or any other eminence near Haifa. In the spring, before it has been parched by the sun, it stretches below, a green carpet, cut across by long lines of pine and cypress, with the dark green of a citrus grove here and there, or the red roofs and white silos of a kibbutz or moshav sheltering among trees.

One admires the view more at a distance than close up, for when one descends and moves among the individual settlements, no matter how one marvels at their achievements, one becomes dazed by their similarity.

Israel has always been short of money and time, and everything she has erected has had to be done in the shortest possible period at the least possible expense, and this has meant ruthless standard-ization. There are outposts of individuality. Jerusalem, in spite of some ugly suburbs, is still immutably itself. Safad and Tiberias retain their distinct character. Nahariyah, near Acre, built by German immigrants before the war, still has the air of a central European watering place. In Savyon, parts of Haifa and Ramat Gan, indi-viduals with money have been able to buy off the town planners and to erect habitations which reflect something of their own taste. These are oases, but in general one is confronted by a stunning sameness.

In Tel-Aviv the old area round Herzl Street with its courtyards and caryatids and palms is being planned out of existence. Its one public building of character, the Herzliya Gymnasium, has been demolished to make room for a multi-storied office-block ('the tallest building between here and Tokyo', one is told), a slotted slab without distinction or character. One will know the newer parts of Tel-Aviv from the older ones, the more prosperous parts from the less prosperous, but within each area the streets look alike and the buildings look alike.

And beyond Tel-Aviv one often gets the feeling that if one has seen one town one has seen the lot; if one has seen one moshav or kibbutz one has seen the lot. In Europe there is usually local build-ing material to distinguish one village from another, or a local church. In Israel most houses are of concrete, and there is also a great deal of prefabrication. And as for synagogues, many settlements are non-religious and need none, and even in the religious villages there is often little to distinguish the synagogue from any other building.

Every part of Israel is rich in antiquities, and in some areas, especially round Caesarea and Ashkelon it is difficult to dig without turning up some remnant of Roman or Crusader times. Each area has its own museum, large or small, with a collection of ancient pottery, coins, ornaments, weapons. Israel is an area which has been traversed by almost every great empire, and following the traces of each is a popular national pastime. The most famous and popular site is of course Masada, but on almost every day of the year one can see parties of school-children scampering among the rocks of Megiddo and Beth Shemes and Tel Lachish and Avdat and a hundred other sites.

This constant sense of the old compensates for the sameness of the new, and the sameness lies in the buildings. The people could not be more varied.

Israelis stem from a hundred different lands and often their very appearance declares their origins. Those who believe there is such a thing as a Jewish type could never have been to the Jewish state. Exile tends to exaggerate the national characteristics in everyone. There are few Englishmen quite as English as those one can see in

Israel. One can still have afternoon tea out of silver tea-pots with tweedy ladies who sigh over the thought that Israel has no Harrods. 'Ell pee topple-you!' I once heard an umpire shout at a cricket game in an 'Anglo-Saxon' kibbutz, most of whose members were born in Germany.

One can get an idea of the heterogeneity of the population if one spends a Sabbath morning in Jerusalem and watches the passing parade. There is little traffic on a Sabbath, the shops and cafés are closed, and once the synagogue services are over, there is little to do except see and be seen, and one may, in the course of a few minutes, encounter a turbaned elder from Yemen, *Chassidim* in their black hats and gaberdines and long side-curls; Romanian immigrants with platinum teeth, and bell-bottom trousers *à la* Khrushchev; ladies in exotic silks and ornate headgear from some remote Persian province; a swarthy pair in striped pyjamas, and the occasional gentleman in a dark suit and even a bowler hat who looks as if he might have been 'something in the City'.

There is an immense variety of headgear indicating not only country of origin, but degree of devoutness. Most Orthodox Jews have their heads covered, but some are more orthodox than others and this will be reflected in the size of the coverage.

The young man from, say, the Mizrachi party, who is religious but modern, will wear a small, knitted coppel about the size of a pancake: if he is less modern, he will wear a large, black silken coppel: if he is a Chassid he will wear a black hat over a black coppel and is thus doubly secure against a bare head. (Some individuals, one should add, wear a cap in bed, others allow themselves to sleep with their head naked.)

(The devout single woman is allowed to go bare-headed, the married one is not. In some cases she will be content with a mere kerchief, but often she will wear a wig either on top of her hair, or will shave her head to do so. The idea behind this is that the modest woman will keep her allurements hidden, but if she is rich her wig may be a good deal more alluring than the hair it hides. If she is poor she will have to content herself with something resembling a door-mat.)

There are streets in Tel-Aviv and Jaffa where the smell of half a dozen types of cooking hangs in the air like a haze, and where one may eat gefulte fish, shish-kebab, couscous, goulash, schnitzel, kalbwurshtel, pâté de foie gras and wimpies.

Each immigrant group has its own exaggerated idea of its place in the national hierarchy. The Russians look down upon the Poles, the Poles upon the Hungarians, the Hungarians upon the Roman-ians; everybody looks down upon North Africans, and the English look down upon everybody else. As for the Germans, they are not looked up at, or down on, but askance at. And each has its anec-dotes about the other. There is the story of the Romanian whore who decided to go straight and became engaged to be married. On the eve of her wedding her conscience began to worry her and she went to a Rabbi to ask whether she should tell her fiancé about her past. 'Yes,' said the sage, 'you should tell him everything.'

'Everything?'

'Well, on second thoughts, everything except the fact that you're Romanian!'

Such anecdotes pass as amiable banter. The differences between the European groups are not taken seriously; the differences between the European and non-European are.

'I have nothing against Moroccans', the Western immigrant will insist, 'only I wouldn't want my daughter to marry one.'

Differences fade with the younger generation. Whatever their national origins the children all have a tendency to be dark, raucous and insolent.

And differences would fade faster but for the *lantsmanschaft* instinct in the Jew. Almost, if not every, group of immigrants has its own association. The Americans have theirs, the British have theirs, as do the Germans, Hungarians and Baltic Jews. Some groups were deliberately settled together in one area by the Jewish Agency, and others, who were scattered, gradually came together. To an extent these associations are mutual-aid societies. They will help with accommodation, schooling, a job. What would be called nepotism elsewhere, and is sometimes referred to as *protectsia* in Israel, is part of this *lantsmanschaft*. It means, of course, that those immigrants whose associates are not in influential positions are at a serious disadvantage. This is one of the grievances of the Sephardim.

Lantzleit tend to congregate not only in the same towns but in the same parts of town, to send the children to the same schools and to patronize – or avoid – the same synagogues.

There is also a hankering after the past, a nostalgia for old scenes. High up on Mount Carmel in the Haifa cafés one can still find elderly ladies with drooping cheeks, eating *Sachertorte*, chattering in German, and sighing for places from which they fled for their lives.

There is also a pride in European culture. That this culture included Auschwitz is overlooked in recollections of Goethe, Schiller, Shakespeare, Milton, Tolstoy, Dante. Hazaz, one of Israel's most eminent writers, complained a few years ago that Israeli young people preferred Balzac to their own classics. In 1966 Israel spent over $3,500,000 on foreign books – all this is quite apart from Hebrew translations of foreign works. There are few Jewish homes without a well-stocked bookshelf, and not all the books are from overseas. There are 65 publishing houses in Israel. In Jerusalem bookshops are as numerous as pubs in Dublin, but even in small towns like Rishon Le Zion one will find at least six booksellers.

The 'people of the Book' are a bookish people, but not everyone is confident that they will always remain so.

Israeli papers are, on the whole, earnest, serious, almost grim, both in their treatment of news and their make-up, but some magazines have hit upon an unexpectedly large market for scandal, bosoms and pornography. *Haolam Hazeh* blazed the way, *Bul* followed but did not get very far, till it had the singular good fortune of being prosecuted for contravening security laws. It is now selling like hot cakes and has found an imitator in *Op*. Besides these, which are weekly magazines, there are other occasional publications which purvey all the salaciousness of Charing Cross Road, without, however, displaying any of its quality of production. British pornography is at least glossy and expensive. The Israeli variety is shoddy and cheap.

Soccer excites wide interest, as do other games, like basket-ball, but it is limited by the fact that Israelis work a 6, or at best 5½ day week. The rest day is the Sabbath and on that day Orthodox Jews, who comprise at least a third of the population, cannot play games nor pay to see them played. The government, and particularly the Histadrut, assist sports clubs in one way or another, but on those occasions when Israeli teams or athletes have appeared abroad they have usually made a poor to derisory showing.

The cinema is by far the most popular form of entertainment. There are nearly 300 cinemas in the country, and the average attendance per head of population is 20 a year. In the small towns the cinemas are the focal points of night life, though discothèques in places as improbable as Rishon Le Zion and Beersheba are beginning to blare in upon them. And they are being seriously threatened by television.

Israel has as yet no television service but television aerials sprout from the rooftops of homes, especially in the north, which cannot yet afford a gas cooker. Some of the sets were brought in by immigrants, but others were bought locally by people who must have paid at least two months' wages for them. And they tune in to Arab stations. Television knows no boundaries. It is this, more than anything else, which has forced the hand of the government, and Israel is soon to have its own television. If the public is to be corrupted, goes the argument, let it be corrupted by indigenous rather than foreign matter.

Israel is still in many ways a paternalistic society. The devout Jew will turn to his sages for guidance on much more than purely religious issues. The secular Jew has retained something of this habit and will often allow the secretariat of his moshav, kibbutz, party or trade union to direct him along the ways of righteousness.

Histadrut enterprises, for example, give their employees an annual allowance which must be spent away from home in a rest centre. If they prefer to stay at home during their holidays, or with relatives, they forfeit their allowance. The Histadrut is anxious that its employees should not only rest, but should actually be seen to be resting.

143

When demands for television began to be heard in the late fifties and early sixties they were fiercely opposed by Ben Gurion and his colleagues. The country could not afford it, they insisted, and it was not good for the country. Thus, even when the Rothschild Trust, a charity foundation deriving funds from the Rothschild family, offered a pilot scheme of television for schools at its own expense, it was probed with suspicion by a doubting Knesset. The scheme is now in operation, and, thanks to the Arabs, it seems likely that the rest of the population will have television before the end of the decade.

The national passion for the cinema, which will no doubt be transferred in due course to television, arises possibly from the escapism inherent in the Jew.

Life in Israel is hard. The working day begins at six for most people (and earlier on the land), and eight in shops and offices. There is a 47-hour week, but many people work a good bit longer to make ends meet, and many salaried employees such as clerks, school-teachers and civil servants take two or three jobs, where they can get them.

Wages are, by Mediterranean standards, high, but their purchasing power is not. A farm labourer may earn about £10 a week, a tractor driver £12, a skilled factory hand £13, a skilled building worker £15, a good secretary £15, a skilled artisan £16, the assistant director general of a Ministry, equivalent in Britain to the Deputy Under Secretary of a Government Department, about £40.

The basic needs are easily met. Housing, in most cases, is subsidized. Bread, fruit, vegetables and eggs are likewise subsidized and inexpensive. One may buy a shirt or a pair of shoes of execrable quality inexpensively, but outer garments are a major investment.

Most Israelis dress shoddily. This is less obvious in the summer when a shirt and a pair of trousers are enough to garb one, and sometimes even a shirt is unnecessary, but in winter, and especially on cold days, one can see the most bizarre ensembles imaginable. In a synagogue one morning I saw an elder in his Sabbath best wearing pointed Italian shoes, blue gaberdine trousers, a black double-breasted jacket with brass buttons, a white muffler and a cloth cap.

A good suit in Israel is almost as expensive as a good suit in Britain and will cost most wage-earners nearly a month's pay. Outside the three towns if one is seen in a jacket with trousers to match, one is pointed out in the street.

If a large family has a small, four-roomed flat it is spaciously accommodated. Most have to be content with three, or even two rooms. Furniture of any but the poorest quality is very expensive, and the poorest quality is not cheap, yet all this has not affected the ability of most Israeli families to accommodate the incessant descent of relatives and friends. At night beds come out from under beds, from settees, from walls, from cupboards, and hallways and kitchens are converted into dormitories. The tradition of hospitality remains unimpared.

Foreign travel, expensive in itself, is punitively taxed, but internal travel is cheap and sometimes costs nothing.

Hitch-hiking, or tremping as it is called locally, is a recognized way of getting around. A pretty girl need never set foot in a public vehicle, but anyone can obtain a lift without much difficulty, and on Friday afternoons there are known points where people queue for a lift as they might queue for a bus.

Bus stations, especially on Friday afternoons, are bedlam, with beggars rattling their cans; vendors shouting their wares; excited mothers trying to marshal miscreant children; buses hooting; infants crying; ducks quacking, hens clucking (for many Israelis prefer to buy their poultry live), and people everywhere in angry argument. Israelis are keen travellers, and although they have but one day free there takes place every Friday afternoon a great trans-migration of souls.

Buses are uncomfortable even when empty. Usually they are packed with passengers standing nose to neck, but they are cheap, and fast to the point of being reckless. As cynics aver, they get you there dead on time.

If the cinema offers one form of escape, and travel another, a third is betting. Israel has a national lottery and football pools, and the latter are threatening to overtake the former. A lottery ticket costs 7s. 6d. and prizes, which may be worth as much as £20,000, are small by British standards, but their following is immense and they form a major industry. Some of the ticket sellers operate from small glass kiosks scattered about the towns, others are itinerant and move among cafés, shops and even offices. And on Friday morning when the results come out there is a crush of punters at every kiosk, checking numbers with a mixture of hope, anxiety and despair.

These scenes give one an idea of the tireless optimism of the Jew. When an Englishman places a bet he *hopes* to win: the Jew who does so *expects* to win, and if he doesn't he feels positively cheated.

It may be that the passion for betting is due to the inability of Israelis to reconcile themselves to the role of mere wage-earners – which the large majority are. Their penchant for enterprise is irrepressible.

It does not take much to be in business in Israel. If one owns a weighing machine one is in business, and one may find such operators scattered about Tel-Aviv offering to gauge one's weight for 3d.

If one has a typewriter one is in business, and one may find such businessmen outside law courts and government offices, with their machines on orange boxes, ready to fill in forms, explain documents, draft petitions. They function substantially as poor men's solicitors.

Those with a ready flow of old clothes or food-parcels from abroad can also be in business. There used to be a man – and he may still be there – on a pitch opposite the general post office in Jerusalem with tinned Hungarian goulash from Cardiff. He never had more than a few tins in front of him, and if he sold one his day was made.

Haulage is a common occupation. Some men begin with their own strong back. The less robust may find themselves a soap box, place it on a pair of roller skates and operate as short distance carriers round the markets. On a slightly more exalted level are the tricycle owners. Beyond them are the men with the donkey carts, and so on, by degrees till one reaches the plutocracy of scooter-drawn vehicles. Yet even with this relentless quest for entrepreneurial openings, only 18 per cent of the working population is self-employed.

There is, of course, a sense in which members of kibbutzim are also self-employed, and they are no less enterprising than the business section of the community, and in some respects more so. The idea that they must confine themselves to agriculture has long since been abandoned. Agriculture may still be their principal occupation, but in many cases it is no longer their principal source of income. They have foundries, factories, workshops, fisheries, canneries, hotels. The individual member may still have to work as hard as ever, and his own private possessions may still be meagre, but he enjoys a standard of living to which many urban dwellers, working every bit as hard, cannot aspire.

That the older kibbutzim like Degania, Kinneret, Afikim, Ein Harod, should be wealthy is only to be expected, but even the newer ones founded since the war are often garden suburbs with wide lawns kept green by the incessant hiss of sprinklers, homes in shaded arbours, flower-beds carefully tended, air-conditioned dining-halls and public rooms, and large swimming-pools.

Their children receive an excellent education up to university level, and if they go on to university their fees and living expenses are met by the kibbutz. Every settlement has a full cultural programme with lectures, film-shows, theatrical performances and concerts, all of them free.

An *élite* is almost necessarily self-proclaimed, but the belief of kibbutzim that they are the *élite* of Israel is shared by many people outside. They nurtured the Jewish army, they were the citadels in the War of Liberation. Their members have risen to the highest offices of state. The Prime Minister was once a member of a kibbutz, the Speaker of the Knesset still is a member.

The kibbutzim contain the landed gentry of Israel, where generation succeeds generation to the same estate, and a young man from a kibbutz may expect a place in the officer corps as naturally as the heir to a baronetcy will expect a commission in the Guards.

The kibbutzim offer a great deal to their members, but demand almost everything of them, and they therefore remain an *élite* which the public is willing to admire rather than emulate.

36 The topography of Israel offers considerable contrasts. The growth of population necessitates experimenting with the cultivation of such arid deserts areas on the southern Negev which occupy almost half of the country.

37 Nomadic tribesmen outside Beersheba. Many such tribes are changing their way of life in favour of permanent settlements.

38 Nazareth was the birthplace of Christ and is a place of Christian pilgrimage. Today a third of the population are Christian and the remainder Arab.

39 Haifa is Israel's main port for trade with the West. Her main eastern outlet is through the Port of Eilat.

40 Tel-Aviv is the commercial, arts and social centre of Israel. The Dan Hotel on the Tel-Aviv seafront is one of the most luxurious in the country.

41 After fifty years of growth Tel-Aviv has all the characteristics of a modern well-planned city.

42 Jerusalem, as opposed to Tel-Aviv, is a city of variety. This is the shopping centre at Mahane Yehuda.

43 Jerusalem, once a city divided between Arab and Israeli ownership. These Arab refugees are being given milk at a UN centre in Jerusalem.

مركز توزيع الحليب و التغذية و الأضافير الدرج

MILK & SUPPL. FEED. CENTRE DARAJ

44 (*left above*) There are numerous racial types in Israel. This woman is a former inhabitant of the old city of Jerusalem.

45 (*right above*) The Druzes are a minority religious sect whose beliefs are secret. This is the chief of the Druze community in Israel.

46 Young orthodox Jews at prayer.

47 Beersheba is rapidly changing into a minor Tel-Aviv, but bedouins with their camels still sell their wares in the streets.

48 The manufacture of cosmetics is one of the many smaller industries which thrive in a modern Israel. This is the Revlon factory in Ashdod.

49 A post-graduate chemist at the Technion, Israel's main centre for higher education and learning.

50 Israel's climate favours the growth of citrus fruits, such as oranges, which are the country's main export.

51 The Jew excels in the manufacture of textiles. This is a wool textile factory at Ramat Gam.

52 Israel produces great talents in the arts. There are numerous dance companies including the Batsheva Dance Company.

53 Marcel Jancu painting in his studio at Ein Hod.

54 The Israel Festival of Music at the Roman Theatre, Caeserea.

11   The economy

ISRAEL HAS CONTRADICTED many economic laws, but if she had ever conformed to economic orthodoxy she should never have come into existence. In terms of plain accountancy Zionism was an extravagance.

The old Yishuv, as we have seen, was content to devote itself to sacred studies, confident in the belief that in the last resort the Lord would provide. And in the last resort – sometimes in the very last resort – He did.

Although Israel is today very much of this world, a wholly secular state, this belief continues to affect economic policy. She defines her priorities first and thinks about paying for them later, in the unstated hope that something will somehow appear to balance the account. And hitherto something always has done – Israeli appeals organized by the Jewish communities in the diaspora; the Israel Bond drive; US government aid; German reparations. Unilateral payments in one form or another have helped to sustain an economy which is still, to a large extent, inherently unviable.

Israel is a small country and, as far as natural physical resources are concerned, a poor one. She is part of the so-called Fertile Crescent which sweeps southwards from Syria, but her fertility has been limited by a shortage of water. She has been able to coax water upwards to the barren hills and downwards to the arid south, but at great expense. Although abutting upon a region rich in oil, her own oil resources are meagre. The oil reserves discovered in what is optimistically referred to as 'Little Texas' between Ashkelon and Beersheba in 1955, yield 188,000 tons a year, or under 10 per cent of Israel's needs. Natural gas deposits discovered at Rosh Zohar, near the Dead Sea, yield the equivalent of a further 18,000 tons. Experiments with solar energy have been of only marginal value. There is no hydro-electric power in Israel, no coal, and the peat found in the Hule area was not available in commercial quantities. The sole source of power is thermo-generated electricity based on imported fuel.[57] (Oil prospecting, however, continues and there is hope that further reserves may be found.)

Israel has virtually unlimited quantities of magnesium chloride, sodium chloride, calcium chloride, potassium chloride, and magnesium bromide in the Dead Sea. The world demand for such products, unfortunately, is not unlimited, and although the deposits themselves are cheaply extracted, the long haul by road to Ashdod and Haifa is expensive. Nevertheless, output of the various products has been thrusting upwards and it is expected that by 1969 a million tons of potash will be sent abroad.

Israel produces some 80,000 tons of super-phosphates a year, and about half a million tons of low-grade copper ore a year are mined at Timna near Eilat. Small quantities of iron ore have been found at Mt Ramim in Galilee. Many of the raw materials needed for the country's huge building industry, including limestone and gypsum, are available locally, as well as commercial quantities of clays and kaolin.

Israel consists of some 8,000 square miles, most of them barren, but large areas which in most countries would be considered unproductive have been made to yield fruit – though at a price, and the price has not always been economic.[58]

The sandy soils of the coastal plain which carry most of Israel's citrus crop have artesian wells, and there are also surplus waters in the Jezreel valley and the Yarkon. In 1955 water was brought from the Yarkon, which rises in the Judean hills, to the northern Negev. In 1965 a much larger scheme carrying water from the Sea of Galilee to the Negev was completed at a cost of $120,000,000.

About 1,000,000 acres have been cultivated, of which 380,000 are under irrigation. Nearly all of Israel's exploitable water resources have been exploited. Plans for a joint US-Israel nuclear desalination project are under consideration, but they are not so advanced as to offer immediate hopes of further expansion.

Under the Mandate, Palestine imported many of her foodstuffs, including meat on the hoof, butter, eggs, grains and flour, from the surrounding countries. The War of Liberation and subsequent Arab boycott threw her back upon her own resources. In 1950, when her population was 1,000,000 she still had to import more than half of her foodstuffs. Today, with an incomparably higher standard of living, she produces 85 per cent of her needs, and gluts have developed in eggs, vegetables, potatoes and dairy produce. Value of agricultural output at 1948–9 prices increased more than six-fold in the first sixteen years of statehood, and agricultural exports more than ten-fold, from $6·5 million in 1949 to $67 million in 1964. The proportion of the population engaged in agriculture has in fact been decreasing and now stands at about 14 per cent. The higher yields are due to constant infusions of capital into agriculture or irrigation schemes, fertilizers, machinery, and more intensified farming, and these, as may be imagined, have involved the heavy use of foreign currency. Of the $3,000,000,000 of foreign capital invested in Israel between 1948 and 1962, some 20 per cent, or $600,000,000 went to agriculture and irrigation.

Fish is the Jew's meat and at one time most of the fish eaten in Israel came from abroad. (During the years of austerity, in fact, *dag fillet* – imported frozen cod – was almost the staple foodstuff.) She now produces most of her own needs, with four trawlers in the Rea Sea and African waters, a further four in the rich Atlantic grounds off South Africa, and smaller craft in coastal waters and the Sea of Galilee. Fish ponds, which cover some 13,000 acres, produced about half of the 20,250 tons caught during 1964–5.[59] It is doubtful whether such an area of land would continue to be used in this way if the owners had to pay the full economic price for both the land and the water.

The rise in industrial output has been less dramatic and in the decade 1955–64 it multiplied almost three-fold. The most rapid advance has been in mining and quarrying, where the growth has been eight-fold. The value of industrial exports jumped from

£82,000,000 in 1958 to £281,000,000 six years later. Local raw materials have been thoroughly exploited. Cotton, which was introduced into Israel only in 1953 and now covers 35,000 acres, supplies the needs of the local textile industry and even yields a small surplus for export. Citrus is used in large quantities in food processing and also for its by-products, but the bulk of Israeli industries depends on imported raw materials. Moreover the home market snaps up 77 per cent of the total output, a large part of which goes towards satisfying immediate consumer needs. Capital goods form about a third of her output. The very growth in her national product has therefore increased the burden of her international indebtedness.

The rise in output was sustained by the rise in population, and in fact during the heavier periods of immigration population increase tended to race ahead of output, thus pushing up prices. As the immigrants became absorbed they went far towards satisfying the demand they created, but in the initial period of mass immigration shortly after the establishment of the state, the process of absorption was slow and the inflationary pressure remorseless. In 1949, Israel's first full year of independence, imports ran to about nine times the level of exports. In 1950 the proportions were 7:1.

It is not that Israel was being extravagant, but to live at all she had to live beyond her means. Heavy defence spending was partly covered by a resort to the printing presses and the issue of Treasury Bills. Similarly the Development Budget, directed towards the absorption of the newcomers, was financed by Land Bonds. And at the same time the outbreak of the Korean War brought a sharp rise in commodity prices. As a result the cost of living index rose from 100 in 1951 to 169 in 1953, and this despite heavy food subsidies. Consumer goods vanished from the shops. Most articles in common demand were severely rationed. There was a thriving black market and a special corps of economic police was formed to fight it. Buses were stopped on the highways, passengers' goods searched, and anyone with, say, an unregistered chicken in his briefcase, had to explain its presence. Meat became an almost unheard-of commodity, except to tourists, who could still obtain a meat meal on payment of hard currency and the submission of their passports. The so-called austerity of Britain's war years was a time of plenty compared to the austerity endured by Israel.

In 1951 the government reformed its fiscal policy and made strenuous efforts to pay for expenditure out of revenue. The Defence Budget, which had been secret and separate, was incorporated (or partly incorporated, for it is still secret) into the ordinary budget. The issue of Land Bonds was stopped. Income Tax was raised. A 10 per cent levy on bank deposits and bank notes was introduced in 1952, and a property levy in the following year. Credit was restricted. All these measures absorbed a great deal of surplus cash, but at the same time numerous controls which had been used to suppress inflation were partly relaxed. And wage-agreements tied to the cost of living index tended to push up prices. By 1955 the index stood at 233, and by 1956 at 250.

During the Mandate the Palestinian Pound had been based on the Pound Sterling but in 1948 Israel was expelled from the sterling area. The fiction of parity with sterling was bravely maintained for a time but it was abandoned in 1952 and a multiple system of exchange rates, varying from ILo·357 to the dollar to ILI to the dollar, was introduced. This was found impractical and eventually a unitary rate of ILI·80 was established.

In the late fifties, as the rate of immigration declined, early investments yielded their first fruits: monetary expansion was slowed down, and the pressure on the economy was eased. But the relief was temporary. Restitution money from West Germany began to be injected into the economy in 1958 and there was a heavy inflow of other unilateral funds. Between 1952 and 1962 prices rose by nearly 164 per cent. The inflationary spiral was in motion again. The trade gap widened.

In 1962, Mr Levi Eshkol, who was then Finance Minister, devalued the currency to IL3 to the dollar. At the same time he voiced the hope that wage increases would not outpace increases in productivity, and that part of the latter would be available to reduce prices.

His hope was not fulfilled. In 1965, the Gross National Product rose by 8–9 per cent, wages by about 15 per cent and prices by 8.

'Everything has been increasing', said Mr Chaim Zadok, the Minister of Trade, Industry and Development, 'our exports are increasing, our imports are increasing and our deficit is increasing'.

There was full employment. The economy was continuing to expand, but the country was making no perceptible progress to-wards her long-term aim of economic independence. And what made this particularly worrying was the fact that a large part of the unilateral funds propping up the economy were transitory.

Israel has benefited greatly from American aid to under-developed countries, but by 1961 she outgrew this category and aid stopped. US technical assistance ended in 1962, and interest on development loans rose progressively from 0·75 per cent in 1962 to 3·5 per cent in 1965. German reparation payments came to an end in 1964.

In 1964 the government published a five-year industrial plan which envisaged an increase in output from IL5,700,000,000 to IL9,900,000,000 within that time, and the doubling of industrial exports. But in view of the deterioration of the trade position a policy of restraint was introduced with the 1965–6 budget. Credit was tightened and investment was made more selective. The trade position improved. In 1966 the trade deficit was cut, and in the latter half of that year prices rose by only 1·2 per cent which, by Israeli standards, is no rise at all.

Investments which had risen to IL3,000,000,000 in 1964, fell to IL2,500,000,000. Immigration fell to a trickle. The construction industry, which had employed almost 10 per cent of the labour force, slumped and one by one other sectors began to feel the pinch. At the end of 1966 the government had to intervene to save Rassco (The Rural and Suburban Settlement Company), one of the largest housing and construction companies in the country, from collapse. By the end of the year there were 96,000 unemployed, or some 10 per cent of the labour force.[60]

Israel's economy has been in a state of crisis from the very begin-ning, only sometimes the crisis has been more critical than others, and it all derived from attempts to achieve numerous irreconcilable aims. The long-term aim, as we have seen, is economic indepen-dence. At the same time Israel has sought to maintain a large and effective fighting force, a continuous flow of immigrants, a high level of social security, an egalitarian distribution of income, full employ-ment and a steady balance of payments. The last was, of course, never within sight, and the distant aim of independence has become very distant indeed.

The full size of the defence budget is not known (the published figure is 21·4 per cent of the national budget) but its effects on the economy are felt everywhere, not only because of the massive expenditure on arms imports, but also because of the calls it makes on the skills and manpower of the community.

Over a million immigrants have entered Israel since 1948. A large proportion of them were without capital or skills, but their integra-tion was assisted by lavish donations from the Jewish communities in the diaspora. Something like $1,600,000,000 has been raised for Israel since 1948 by the United Jewish Appeal of America alone. Immigrants were thus provided with ready spending power and instead of depressing the economy they made it more buoyant, too buoyant in fact.

The idea of social security is one point where Jewish tradition and socialist theory meet (there are a few others); the extensive welfare system built up by the Histadrut and augmented by the state and various private foundations, compares well with that available even in the wealthy countries of western Europe. The system is perhaps a little too secure, for it is difficult and expensive to dismiss even a very inefficient employee in Israel, and there have been complaints that the zeal and industry shown by earlier immigrants have been less evident among the later ones.

The principle of egalitarianism is still a basic element in economic policy. The Histadrut in particular is determined to see that the worker gets a constant share of the national cake, even if it means that the cake as a whole may shrink. The basic wage of many Israelis bears little relation to the sums they actually earn, for there are all sorts of family allowances, cost of living allowances and other fringe benefits.

The cost of living allowances rise with the cost of living index. Such allowances do not and cannot guarantee a worker's real income – but only his share of whatever is going. 'Guarantee' is perhaps too strong a word, for such allowances help to accelerate inflation and endanger the whole economy. Yet, at the end of 1966, with a tenth of the labour force out of work, the Histadrut continued to press for them. At the same time, individual employers, threatened with a shut-down because of the drop in orders, were successfully negotiating wage-cuts, and workers at the huge Leyland assembly works in Ashdod agreed to a cut of 15 per cent.

Though Israel is poor in physical resources, especially when set against the standard of living to which she presumes, her greatest natural asset is the ingenuity of her own people; and this, when combined with brute hard work (as it has been in the past), can achieve, indeed has achieved, remarkable results.

During the Mandate the low figures which Britain consistently placed on the absorptive capacity of Palestine – and which were as consistently challenged by the Jewish Agency – were not part of a conspiracy to keep the Jews out, but genuine appraisals based on concrete evidence. The Zionists, however, showed that even the most inhospitable lands could be opened up, given sufficient zeal, application and capital.

Another example is the diamond industry. Israel has no diamonds, but she has a large labour force (nearly 7,000 people) skilled in the treatment of diamonds. She imports the stones rough and sends them out polished, and in 1964 they brought in $138,000,000 (gross).

Israelis can sometimes be a little too confident in their ability. Witness the attempt to build up an instant sea-carrying trade – and this by a people not only without a maritime tradition but almost proverbially land-bound. (To this day a devout Jew who has crossed the seas – even the English Channel – will offer up a special prayer for having emerged safely from great danger.)

The textile field is one in which Jews may claim certain expertise, but expertise is not enough. Something may be gained from her enterprising fashion industry, but the textile industry as a whole, even though it earned $40,000,000 in exports in 1964, was built up more with an eye to finding employment outlets for new immigrants than the state of the market. The same may be said of her vehicle assembly plants, though in this case there are also security considera-tions involved.

Israel believes that it is infinitely better to use public money to subsidize an industry than to keep men on the dole, but by creating artificial employment she is keeping wages at an artificially high level, and limiting the opportunities for real employment.

The export of citrus goods brought in nearly $53,000,000 in 1964, and other agricultural products $14,000,000. The latter, especially the export of off-season vegetables, could be greatly expanded but for the fact that Israel is competing in these products with low-wage areas.

The climate, the sheer beauty and variety of the land, its historical associations, the tug of sentiment, have combined to make Israel a major tourist centre. In 1964 some 300,000 tourists brought in $54,000,000. Although second only to diamonds in its foreign exchange income, the tourist trade is in fact the more important because a comparatively small part of its costs are incurred in foreign currency. Tourists are advancing eastwards along the Mediterranean shore. To the British traveller, for example, Greece is becoming what Italy used to be. Israel is almost next in line.

The Government Tourist Industry Development Corporation has lent over IL60,000,000 to various hotels, restaurants and recommended shops in the past nine years, and it is making further sums available at the rate of nearly IL10,000,000 a year. The valley of the Dead Sea, with its numerous mineral springs, is being developed as a winter resort, and there have been rapid develop-ments too at Eilat, which has its own development corporation. Distance is becoming less of a handicap as the cost of travel declines, and Israel is almost ideally equipped for the growing number of travellers who now take two holidays a year. Wages form a painfully high part of the costs of the tourist industry, but if they could be kept in check there is no reason why Israel should not attract as many as 750,000 tourists within the next decade. It is the one industry where, wage structure apart, Israel has a natural advantage, and which has yet to be fully exploited.

The government offers special inducements to investors willing to set up industries in development areas, and especially to those with foreign capital. Grants are available to cover up to 80 per cent of the cost of plant, as well as high depreciation allowances; relief from property taxes for up to ten years; reduced tax rates for both companies and individuals; exemption from custom duties and purchase tax on materials required to set up the undertaking. The government also helps to provide factory sites and housing and makes grants of up to IL1,500 per worker for the training of labour. Non-resident investors can transfer all their profits in their own currency and, after a time, their capital. In 1964 foreign investment totalled $174,000,000, which is a flea bite when set against the sums needed.

The government itself is a heavy investor, not for doctrinal reasons, but because of the paucity of private capital and the non-commercial nature of many of the projects which the government is anxious to promote. In general, public money goes where private enterprise and the Histadrut fear to tread, like the Timna copper-mines. Where the government can find a private buyer for its holdings, it will dispose of them. Thus Israel has in recent years witnessed a process of de-nationalization, and the Haifa oil refineries, 65 per cent of the stock of Palestine Potash (which owns the Dead Sea works) and numerous other public assets, have been sold to private buyers.

Private enterprise in Israel accounts for about 58 per cent of the net domestic product. The rest is divided almost equally between the government and the Histadrut.

The basic problem of Israel, like that of Britain, is an inability to live within her means. This is partly due to her crippling defence burden; but she also aspires to a Western standard of living on what is an Eastern income. When the slump at the end of 1966 and early in 1967 brought the prospect of a levelling off in prices and wages, the government became nervous of the level of unemployment and began injecting money into the economy – money derived not from any actual or prospective revenues, but artificially created.

In April it began the payment of an unemployment dole for the first time. Loans were made available for house repairs at generous rates and the budget estimates made it inevitable that there would be a further spate of deficit financing, an upsurge in prices, and so until the next time. The immediate problem of unemployment would be solved, but the fundamental problem of the imbalance of trade would be aggravated. The trade gap of about $500,000,000 a year was narrowing, but it seemed likely that it would widen again in 1967.

Then suddenly the trouble on the borders, with which Israel had learned to live as one learns to live with rheumatism, escalated into war. The unemployed disappeared, but the economy came to a halt, and all the plans and careful calculations became null.

The amount of actual physical damage suffered by Israel in the six days' war was slight, but the economic disruption was tremendous and it is estimated that mobilization was costing the country $3,000,000 a day. Some of this will no doubt be made good by contributions from Jewish communities abroad, which are expected to total some $300,000,000, but it must add to the burden of indebtedness and exacerbate a situation already sufficiently grave.

But against this must be set the imponderables of Israeli life. One of the reasons for the economic slump was that Israeli workmen were becoming more prone to ease off, to strike, to demand more pay for less work – in short, to behave like workmen elsewhere. And not only workmen. The spirit of idealism which had propelled the whole country was becoming spent. Israel felt that she had earned the right, as *Time* magazine put it, to live a little. Idealism, indeed, was giving way to cynicism.

Then came the war, and the spirit which had enabled her to overcome her earlier difficulties returned. She was like a nation regalvanized. It was a sensation Britain experienced during Dunkirk and which she has been trying to summon up again since. If Israel should be able to show, in peace, the ingenuity and determination she showed in war, her prosperity is assured.

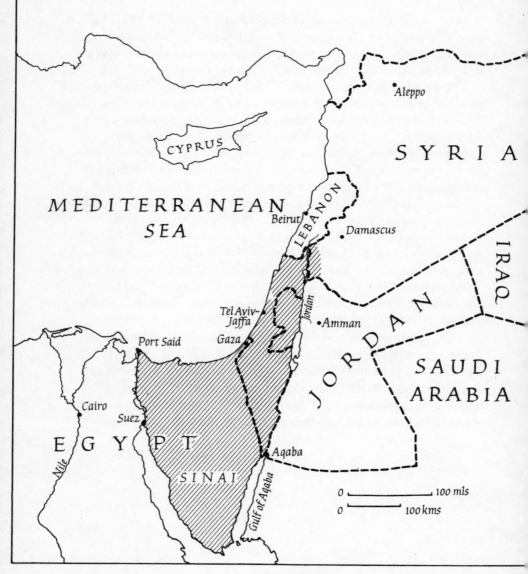

Israel and her neighbours

12   Foreign policy

THROUGHOUT HER NINETEEN YEARS of existence Israel's main concern has been to see how far one can live in a state of war with one's neighbours without being actually involved in fighting. The answer has been, hardly at all. In those nineteen years she has been involved in innumerable skirmishes and two bloody campaigns.

The fundamental fact of her foreign policy is that the Arabs have not recognized her right to exist, and have done everything by boycott, blockade, harassment and, finally, outright aggression to make her existence impossible.

Israel is in part a creation of the United Nations, but after having declared, in November 1947, that there should be a Jewish state, the UN did nothing to prevent the Arabs from trying to stifle it at birth. Nor did the UN take any steps against Egyptian defiance of its resolutions on the freedom of passage through the Suez Canal; and it was only after the Israeli army blasted its way down to Sharm el-Sheik in 1956 that Israel obtained freedom of shipping in the Gulf of Aqaba. And then only for a while.

The UN Emergency Force which had been placed at Sharm el-Sheik after the Sinai campaign was withdrawn at the behest of President Nasser in May 1967 and the blockade reimposed. Israel once again had to take to military action to protect a right which the UN could only affirm but not assure.

Her experience of May and June 1967, when the nations who had never lifted a finger in her hour of need rushed in to counsel her in her hour of triumph, must have made her doubt whether there was anything positive to be hoped for from the UN at all.

Israel's foreign policy, as we shall see, has to an extent been motivated by certain lofty ideals, but it is basically tied up with her security needs and a concern to ease her sense of encirclement.

It was security rather than a passion for reconciliation which was the reason for Ben Gurion's policy of friendship with West Germany. There was a moment early in 1965 when this policy was shaken, when Germany, bowing to a threat that Egypt would recognize the Ulbricht régime, suspended arms shipments to Israel and offered economic aid instead. On 15 February the Knesset expressed 'astonishment and indignation' and Mr Eshkol told West Germany that her policy towards Israel was 'the touchstone for her aspiration to find her place in the family of nations.' An amicable settlement was, however, reached and later in the year Israel and West Germany established full diplomatic relations.

The active support given by Nasser to Algerian rebels helped to bring Israel and France nearer together. The French, even before the Second World War, partly out of a desire to embarrass Britain, had allowed the Zionists to maintain kibbutz training centres in Syria, and after the war they had kept a blind eye on the movement of illegal immigrants. In 1956, when the supply of Czech arms to Egypt had seriously upset the balance of power, France supplied Israel with 24 Mystère IV fighters and a quantity of other equipment; and a secret pact with France later that year enabled her to launch the Sinai operation.

France has since continued to supply Israel with arms, and the planes which shattered the Arab air forces and made Israel's victory inevitable in the six days' war were French.

Israel was also able to enjoy the overwhelming sympathy of all sections of the French public except the extreme left, and in the first days of June 1967 the streets of Paris, a city in which antisemitism is endemic, milled with crowds shouting their support for the Jewish state. But the government kept itself aloof from either side, and when the fighting stopped it came down vehemently against Israel, as if somehow affronted by the very scale of Israel's triumph.

Israel has been running a sort of poor man's Colombo Plan for the less-developed areas of the world. She was, until recently, such an area herself, and is a prime example of what outside capital with native determination and ingenuity can achieve. She has much to teach from her own immediate experience, and she cannot be thought of as an old colonialist exploiter in a mood of atonement. States seeking her help could do so without any feeling of being patronized. Thus between 1958 and 1966 well over 7,000 trainees from over 90 countries in Africa, Asia, Latin America and the Mediterranean Basin have taken part in study missions and training courses in Israel.

In 1964 there were 700 experts from Israel in 55 developing states under the auspices of UN agencies or at the invitation of the states concerned. Joint construction, irrigation, shipping, civil engineering and foreign trade companies have been launched with numerous African and Asian states. In recent years Israel has signed agreements for technical cooperation with Brazil, Chad, Colombia, Costa Rica, Dominica, Ghana, the Philippines, Rwanda, Sierra Leone, Togo, Turkey. The International Conference on the Role of Science in the Advancement of New States held in Rehovot in August 1960 arose out of Israel's desire to explore every means of advancing her development, and to share the results of her exploration. In March 1961, 64 students from 24 countries graduated from the first course of the Afro-Asian Institute in Tel-Aviv.

There is obvious self-interest in all these measures. Trade follows aid. Africa, and especially East Africa, as well as some Asian states, would be a natural outlet for an industrialized Negev, and specialized knowledge is in itself an important invisible export. Israel, with her hunger for learning and her rapidly expanding institutes for higher studies, will be, if she is not already, producing more graduates than she can absorb in her own economy, and the less-developed countries could be an important outlet for their skills.

Yet with the self-interest there is an important element of idealism. Israel has always looked upon herself as far more than a refuge for those Jews who could not settle elsewhere. She is a country with a sense of mission whose terms she has not been quite able to define, especially as it affects her relationship with the Jewish world. With the non-Jewish world, however, it is less complex, and her plans to help her less-developed contemporaries are part of a desire to act, even if her resources hardly permit it, as the universal good samaritan.

But there have been disappointments, especially in Asia. In 1955 Arab pressure kept Israel out of the Bandung Conference of Asian and African states.

In 1961 the Casablanca Conference of African states denounced Israel as 'an instrument in the service of imperialism and neo-colonialism not only in the Middle East, but also in Africa and Asia', and the Afro-Asian People's Solidarity Conference in Tanganyika in February 1963 condemned 'Zionist colonialism', and 'Zionist infiltration into Africa'.

In the 1967 crisis India and Tanzania supported Egypt's stand against Israel, and when the fighting was over and the issue came before the UN, a large number of so-called non-aligned states backed a hostile Yugoslav resolution which would have required Israel to withdraw *unconditionally* to her pre-war frontiers. The resolution failed to get the necessary two-thirds majority, but the vote made observers wonder how much of Israel's hopes to become a major force among the non-aligned states was wishful thinking.

The fact is that most non-aligned states are generally aligned with Russia, against America and, as the UN voting showed, against Israel.

The great tragedy of Israel's foreign policy is the failure — and it is certainly not due to any lack of good will on her part — to reach any sort of lasting understanding with the Soviet Union.

The USSR was the rock on which the Nazi might was finally shattered. To many Jews she was *the* liberator, and in 1948 she was among the first to recognize the Jewish state. Moreover, a large part of Israel's kibbutz movement, and numerous individuals among her politicians, were ideologically inclined towards the USSR; without accepting the full implications of Marxism, they felt that the Soviet system was socially the most just and the only viable one for Israel. They also sympathized more with Soviet Russia's foreign policy than with America's. But their sympathy was unrequited.

55 Ben Gurion hoped that the Eichmann trial would create an opportunity for the young people of Israel to acquaint themselves with the tragic Jewish past.

56 Adolf Eichmann was charged, tried, and executed in Jerusalem. Austrian demonstrators protested that he should have been tried in their country.

EICHMAN of GRATZ
BLOODHOUND of GHETTO VILNO!

57 The Israeli voter is faced with a bewildering choice of parties at any general election. This amalgam of posters was for the elections to the sixth Knesset in 1965.

58 The Knesset is Israel's constituent assembly and is elected for a period of five years. Parliamentarians from more than forty legislatures attended the opening of the new Parliament building in 1966.

59 David Ben Gurion, Chairman of the Knesset and Prime Minister of Israel until his retirement in 1963.

60 Levi Eshkol, Israel's Prime Minister, greeting victorious Israeli troops in the Gaza strip after the rout of the Egyptians during the 1967 war.

61 General Moshe Dayan, Commander of Israel's army in 1956 inspecting Israeli troops during the Sinai campaign. He was recalled during the 1967 war as Israel's Defence Minister.

62 A strong fighting force in the Hagana (Israel army) are the women's corps.

63 During the 1967 war jubilant Israeli troops drove through Bethlehem which
was captured from Jordan. The troops took great care not to damage the holy
places in the course of the fighting.

64 The heaviest fighting in the six-day war of June 1967 took place in the old city
of Jerusalem. Israeli troops pause during a break in the battle.

65 There are numerous shrines of Christianity in Israel though Christians form a religious minority. This is a priest of the Greek orthodox Church of St Elijah on Mount Tabor.

66 Primary education in Israel is free. These young orthodox children are being taught in the traditional type of 'Charder' common in Eastern Europe.

67 The majority of the Arab population in Israel is Muslim. This is the Great Mosque of Ahmad-al-Jazzar in Akko which was built during the eighteenth century.

68 The Technion (Israel Institute of Technology, Haifa) is the oldest institute of higher learning in Israel. Graduates receiving their degrees.

69 Jewish pilgrims from Israel and abroad ascend Mount Zion in Jerusalem during one of the three annual Pilgrimage festivals (Passover, Shavuoth and Succoth). In ancient times harvest offerings were brought to the holy sanctuary in Jerusalem.

70 Soldiers and civilians flock to the Wailing Wall, Judaism's most sacred shrine, after the capture of Old Jerusalem in June 1967.

The Slansky trial in Czechoslovakia, in which Jews were charged with conspiring to advance 'world Zionism' and 'Jewish cosmo‍politanism'; the 'Doctors' plot' in Moscow; the supply of Soviet arms to Egypt and Syria; Russia's threat to Israel after Sinai; her support of Nasser in the 1967 crisis and her vituperation against Israel, even to the extent of comparing her to Nazi Germany at the United Nations – all these events have shown clearly and finally that the hostility was no passing phenomenon but a decided part of Soviet foreign policy.

During the six days' war the USSR and all the communist states save Romania broke off diplomatic relations with Israel. What has made this rupture particularly painful is the fact that there are nearly 3,000,000 Jews in the Soviet Union, for many of whom Israel is a light beyond their darkness. They may not, of course, indulge in any form of Zionist activity, but they have tended to use religious occasions – and these are still permitted – to demonstrate their solidarity with the Jewish people.

It is possible that the very depth of feeling which the idea of Israel instils in her Jewish population has startled the Soviet leaders, and they may have hoped that an Arab victory would ease a domestic problem of increasing gravity.

Israel's relations with the United States have – with the exception of the unhappy interlude at the time of Suez – always been parti‍cularly close, and for obvious reasons. The United States has nearly 6,000,000 Jews, the largest, most influential, most prosperous Jewish community in the world: there are as many Jews in metropolitan New York itself as in the whole of Israel. Very few of them have emigrated to Israel, and there is no prospect that any sizeable number of them will, but without their moral, material and political support, the Jewish state could never have come into existence, or continued to exist. The United States has been pumping millions of dollars into Israel, but, unlike the millions which she has applied in most other places, the results have been extremely fruitful and Israel has become a showplace of what economic and technical aid, if properly used, can do.

The United States has tried to get Jews and Arabs to cooperate on at least a technical level and has had a limited success in a unified plan, worked out by the late Eric Johnson, for sharing the water of the Jordan.

Israel looks upon herself as the defender of world Jewry, and its spokesman, a role which not every Jewish community in the diaspora is willing to acknowledge. The Eichmann trial was based on this assumption. When a swastika-daubing incident in Cologne in the winter of 1959 was followed by a rash of swastikas all over Europe, the Israel government dispatched notes to the countries affected expressing her 'shock and concern'.

This role can sometimes conflict with her other ambitions. Thus in November 1962, her vote at the United Nations to support sanctions against South Africa seriously embarrassed the Jewish community of that country, especially as the benevolent attitude of the Union towards Israel has been a good deal more consistent than those of most Afro-Asian states.

13   The Arab minority

IN 1947 WHEN THE OPENING SKIRMISHES of the Arab-Jewish war were being fought, the more prosperous Arab families began to move out of Palestine, as they had done during the 1936–8 troubles. Early in 1948 a wholesale exodus began and by the time the first armistice was signed a year later, of about 700,000 Arabs who had inhabited the Jewish-held areas of Palestine, only 170,000 remained.

Since then about 30,000 Arabs who fled have been allowed to rejoin their families, but more particularly there has been a rapid natural increase. The Arab death-rate has fallen from 15–20 per thousand before 1948 to 6·4 in 1964. The birth-rate is as high as ever, 44 per thousand, three times the Jewish rate. Today there are some 290,000 Arabs in Israel, about 70 per cent of them Moslem, 20 per cent Christian and 10 per cent Druze, and they form 11 per cent of the population.[61]

The Israel Declaration of Independence, elaborated in a government policy statement in 1951, assured 'the Arab minority . . . full and complete equality of rights and obligations in the civic, political, economic, social, cultural, and every other sphere'.

Arabs could vote for the Knesset and seek election to it, and there are seven Arab members in the fifth Knesset. Arabic may be used in the Knesset, and in the courts and in public petitions, and stamps, coins and banknotes bear Arab inscriptions.

The government has financed irrigation and land reclamation in Arab areas, introduced modern mechanical methods and trained

Arab farmers to employ them, with the result that Arab agricultural productivity has multiplied six-fold since 1948.

There are one daily, two weekly and seven periodical papers in Arabic and there is an Arab programme on Kol Israel, the national broadcasting service.

There are about 56,000 Arab pupils in 347 state schools and kindergartens, and a further 12,000 in independent, mostly religious, schools. There are about 250 Arab students in the Hebrew University and Haifa Technion.

A five-year IL70,000,000 plan, which was recently completed, has brought improved water and electricity supplies to Arab villages, and provided better roads, more housing, and new jobs in industry, agriculture and trade.

On the face of it, therefore, Arabs have been making great strides socially, economically, in health, education and welfare; but they still suffer from a great deal of discrimination, petty harassment and a sense of injustice.

Arabs were admitted into the Histadrut in 1953, and allowed to make use of the *Kupat Holim* and the mutual aid institutions, but they were not allowed to vote, nor to elect their own executive officers, nor to run labour councils in Arab areas. They had separate labour exchanges, and they felt that these were used to discriminate against them. At a meeting of the Haifa Labour Council in December 1958, there were complaints that not a single job had been offered that year to the Arab labour exchange in the town, and only one Arab had been hired through the exchange in 1957.[62]

In 1959 labour exchanges, which had been run by the Histadrut, were nationalized. At the same time Arabs were admitted to full membership of the Histadrut.

Until 1959 the daily lives of most Arabs were hedged around with all sorts of restrictions, which made it difficult for them to travel from their villages, change their jobs, alter their place of domicile, or even, in some cases, search after a stray animal.

Arab areas were governed under emergency regulations inherited from the Mandate. Military courts had the right to hold summary trials, hear evidence in secret, and deliver verdicts which could not be questioned. Warrants for arrest could be made out by any army or police officer. The military governors could impose restrictions on movement and employment, and any individual could be detained for up to a year without trial, or ordered to remain in a certain place and report periodically to the police.

These powers were on occasion used to move Arabs from areas where they might be a security risk, and there have been times when the authorities seemed less concerned with security – an expression which can always be used to cover a multitude of sins – than with a desire to grab hold of Arab lands.

In 1951 Arabs living in towns with a Jewish majority were freed from restrictions, but they remained in force elsewhere and affected 90 per cent of Israel's Arabs.

It was not that the restrictions in themselves, given the limited mobility of an Arab villager, were painfully severe, but their application could be arbitrary. No one enjoyed a travel permit as of right, and if the military authorities withheld it, they were under no obligation to give reasons; an Arab who protested too loudly, or too often, or who otherwise displeased the local commander, could be immobilized. 'The case for military rule began to rest on a vicious circle', a student of the Arab minority has written. 'It fed the resent-ment which became its chief justification.'[63]

In August 1959 the restrictions were eased. In the Negev, Arabs were able to come into Beersheba without a permit twice a week instead of once. In northern and central areas they were allowed to travel by day to regional and district centres without a permit alto-gether. School trips could be made right across the country on a collective permit instead of individual ones.

In 1966 restrictions were further eased. Twenty thousand Bedouin who had been confined to a defined zone of the Negev were allowed to move into other parts of the country without permit, and some 60,000 Arabs living in the 'little triangle' abutting on the Jordanian border were also given greater freedom of movement.

At the end of 1966 military government was abolished, and with the exception of some 500 villagers who almost straddle the

Israel-Jordan border, Arabs were permitted to move about Israel without impediment.

The emergency regulations, however, have not been repealed. The basic fact remains that Israel is still technically – and, on occasion, practically – at war with her neighbours. The mass of her Arab population, in the event of an Arab victory in the six days' war, would have quite naturally greeted Arab troops as liberators. At the same time it must be added that while the crisis was at its height the Israeli Arabs posed no grave security problem and a number of them even demonstrated to be allowed to serve in the Israeli army.

The capture of the Gaza strip and the west bank of Jordan brought another 1,250,000 Arabs (including 800,000 refugees) under Jewish rule, and even if it is true that nearly 200,000 have since fled over the Jordan, the remaining number – especially with the high Arab birth-rate – is far too large to be digested in a state which is anxious to remain Jewish.

Apart from annexing the Old City of Jerusalem and certain rectifications to make her frontiers more secure, there is little prospect that Israel will incorporate any large part of the territories she has taken. In the new situation she may also feel sufficiently self-confident to readmit at least some of the Arab refugees, but this must depend less on security considerations than the rate of Jewish immigration.

Postscript

NO DISCUSSION of any aspect of Israeli life is free of a reference to the security problem.

The security problem is omnipresent and urgent and if Israel should be caught in a moment of weakness all that has been achieved in the past seventy years could vanish in a week.

Yet there is a sense in which security is among the least of her problems, for she is aware of the extent of the challenge, and what steps have to be taken to meet it, and on the occasions when her defences have been tested they have not been found wanting.

But security carries secondary and tertiary problems. The sheer weight of the economic burden (published figures tell one little but defence is believed to consume about a third of her national income) means that Israel cannot even hope to become economically independent in the foreseeable future. The yearly traffic of cabinet ministers on fund-raising missions to the Jewish communities in the diaspora will have to continue. The fact that Israel has a fundamental moral claim to their help is beside the point. After seven decades of Zionist endeavour, Zion is still not free of the taint of *Haluka*. The relationship between giver and receiver has never been a wholesome one, and it has affected the attitude of the Israeli to the Jew in the outside world.

Israel means a great deal to the Jew in the diaspora. This was dramatically demonstrated when, for a terrible moment in June 1967, Israel seemed threatened with extinction. While the crisis was at its height Jews all over the world forsook their normal occupations to rush to their transistors at half-hourly intervals. Youngsters, and some who were not so young, milled round the Israeli embassies and thronged the Jewish Agency buildings to volunteer for service. In Britain alone £9,000,000 was raised on behalf of Israel in a matter of days. A tobacconist in Wembley gave his shop. Young brides gave their engagement rings. A housewife in Stoke Newington gave the £400 she had been saving up for a kitchen. Boys at a Jewish public school volunteered to go on bread and water so that the meal money could be sent to Israel. On the Saturday before the fighting, synagogues which were usually half empty were packed for services of intercession, and were packed again the following week for thanksgiving. The feeling of Jewish solidarity was never so complete.

There is hardly a Jew, no matter how slight his belief in Zionism, who does not take pride in the achievements of Israel, and who does not walk more erect for her existence.

This feeling is not always reciprocated. There is among many Israelis a desire, possibly unconscious, to write off the diaspora.

The pioneers of the Second and Third Aliya who settled in Palestine in the first decades of this century, and who founded the kibbutz movement and the labour movement, wanted to create a new society and a new Jew—without the bowed head, the passivity, the distaste for manual labour. They succeeded in both aims, but it was perhaps inevitable that the new Jew should have acquired a distaste for the old.

The pioneers, while they disowned the ghetto and much that it stood for, were aware of its positive side, its warmth, the wealth of its cultural life. They retained their sense of kinship; there were abundant family links. Most of these ended with the Nazi holocaust. And it is not only the fact that European Jewry has perished which has weakened links; it is the way in which it perished.

The pioneers blamed the Jewish faith for the stultification of Jewish life, and they were determined not only to discard Jewish tradition, they almost made a creed out of their very secularism. Jehovah was given no place in the new socialist commonwealth. Israel's Declaration of Independence refers to the 'Rock of Israel' but not God.

188

Now the pioneers were at least sustained by the feeling that they were creating a new order and were part of the inexorable progress of socialism, and all about them bloomed the fruits of their achievements. But since then a generation has grown to maturity who never knew the Sharon when it was not an orchard or the Emek when it was not a garden, and at a time of disenchantment, if not with socialism, then at least with the home of socialism. Their grandfathers cut them off from their old faith, and they are not wholly secure in their new one.

The more recent immigrants, those who stemmed from oriental countries, are in a more difficult situation. The large majority of them were devout, Orthodox Jews. Their children are a good deal less so, but not because they have been attracted by the Messianic secularism of the left-wing groups. They have merely lapsed.

It is by no means certain that every nation needs a creed to sustain it, and all this would be of no significance if Israel was content to be, say, a bustling, dynamic Lebanon.

And there are groups in Israel who would like her to be just that. They call themselves the Canaanites and argue that links with world Jewry are neither necessary nor wholesome and can only be artificially maintained, and that Israel is a Levantine state with precisely the same interests as others in the area. They make no claim upon the Jewish people, and feel the Jewish people has none upon them.

The Canaanites are a tiny and not, as yet, significant minority, but they are articulate and their views have a certain logical consistency which is not always apparent in the ceaseless rhetoric of Israeli politics.

Israel is a nation obsessed with a sense of mission. Most of her leaders may not be religious, but she still thinks in prophetic terms of 'being a light unto the nations'.

Israel, they believe, has saved herself by her exertions, and she could save the world by her example.

And the example, Ben Gurion felt, was a self-invigorating *Chalutziut*, a constant re-evocation of the pioneering spirit. Hence his dramatic move to Kibbutz Sde Boker, in the Negev, in 1953. He had visions of a new generation emerging sand-blasted by the wilderness as an earlier generation had been purged by the malarial swamps of the Emek.

It was a theory of the continuing challenge, but young Israel did not respond to it, or at least not in sufficient numbers. The Negev is being settled, but in the old familiar ways, by higher wages, by grants, by subsidies, by tax incentives.

There are in the whole of Israel today some 800 rural settlements, of which 230, with a population of 81,000, are kibbutzim. They are the bed-rock on which the state rests, but they form only about 3 per cent of the population, and they are a diminishing minority.

Israel today is substantially a western country, with western tastes and western values, the same careerism, the same grim determination to make ten cents grow where five grew before, and, if anything, an even greater tendency for the individual to get locked in the grip of machines. This is not to deny that there are large islands of altruism. One recalls, to give a recent example, the readiness of the Hebrew University staff to forgo a salary increase because of the economic crisis. But the fact that so much of the economy is in cooperative hands has meant that individual greed has been replaced by the collective sort. The kibbutzim, for all the selflessness of their individual members, did not hesitate to lay their hands on Arab lands whenever the opportunity arose. The Histadrut, which has come to think of itself as the second, if not the first, estate and to believe that what's good for the Histadrut is good for Israel, has consistently pushed wage levels beyond the point which the economy could afford.

If the spirit of *Chalutziut* built the country, and sustained it through the ordeals of war, it does not altogether typify the spirit of the new Israel.

And even *Chalutziut* has its negative side. The pioneer is to some extent a visionary, and visions tend to be particular.

It is difficult to explain in terms of British politics why Israel should have three Labour parties, Mapai, Mapam and Ahdut Avoda, why the Hapoel Hamizrachi should be linked with Mizrachi rather than Mapai, and why there should be four distinct kibbutz organizations, and why there should be three religious parties, rather than one, struggling for a Torah state. Such factional- ism arises out of more than an inability to compromise, but the feeling of each group that it is the depository of revealed truth. Idealism often dissipates the very energies it releases.

If the new creeds have been found wanting is there anything to be hoped for from a revival of the old?

About 15 per cent of the country votes for the religious parties, yet about 40 per cent of the children go to religious schools. An election involves more immediate issues than an education, but the attraction of the religious schools alone shows that religion remains a powerful force, and there are other facts to confirm it. A good part of the ideological Aliya of recent years has consisted of people who have settled in Israel for religious reasons, even though it has involved them in considerable material sacrifice. Aliya, to the truly devout Jew, is a religious obligation, and in religious circles the question of the alienation of the Israeli from the diaspora Jew does not arise; the unity of Israel is a fundamental article of the Jewish faith.

Yet the religious groups in Israel have never fully worked out what their role in a Jewish state should be. At the one extreme stand the Neturei Karta, who believe that the Zionists have usurped the functions of the Messiah and who do not recognize the Jewish state. Then there is the Aguda which does sit in the Knesset but which, since 1952, has not been allowed by its Rabbis to hold government office. The Poalei Aguda, more venturesome still, is both in the Knesset and in the government. The Mizrachi and Hapoel Hamizrachi, which constitute the National Religious Party, have been part of every coalition since the beginning of the state.

All the parties insist that the laws of Israel should be based on the Torah, but none, possibly with the perfect faith that they would never be required to implement it, has ever worked out what this would involve. The Torah itself is comparatively permissive, but the myriad of observances tagged on to it throughout the centuries and codified in the *Shulkah Aruch* are also accepted as authoritative, and these could paralyse any society which tried to live up to them. But what makes them really impossible is the fact that though Rabbis may add to the observances or prohibitions, they may abrogate none. The best they can do is to 'reinterpret' them so as to make them practicable. Thus, for example, according to Jewish law, all land must lie fallow every seventh year. One can imagine what such a law could do to the economy of a farming community if adhered to. At the beginning of this century a Lithuanian sage published an interpretation of the law which enabled religious farmers to get round it. Poalei Aguda, which has two kibbutzim, does not accept the interpretation and it has been experimenting with hydroponics. And ultra-Orthodox Jews refuse to buy produce grown on Jewish settlements during the sabbatical year.

Similarly, the ultra-Orthodox, when travelling by sea, do not use Jewish vessels because their crews work on the Sabbath.

How would the public services function on the Sabbath in a Torah state? Would all vehicles be banned, and all planes grounded? How would the mercantile marine operate? Would all ships have to dock or drop anchor on the Sabbath? Would power stations stop? Would steel furnaces be banked? Would oil refineries be shut off?

At present the traditional Feast Days are treated as national holidays and Saturday is the official day of rest; on these days there is no public transport in Jerusalem or Tel-Aviv, but in Haifa, where religious Jews form a smaller proportion of the community, there is public transport. Taxis operate all the time, and the individual who cannot get a bus but cannot afford a taxi may hitch a lift on one of the many lorries which virtually function as an auxiliary public transport system on the Sabbath and religious holidays.

The Sabbath is usually strictly observed by those government departments which have been or are under a Minister from one of the religious parties.

There is naturally no post on the Sabbath, but neither are there any special delivery services, nor telegrams.

Jewish laws are comparatively permissive where there is a danger to health and there are therefore no difficulties about operating ambulance services on the Sabbath, but when the Ministry of Health was a religious fief nurses who had to take notes on the

Sabbath were instructed to write with their left hand if they were right-handed, and vice versa.

The Rabbinical courts have jurisdiction over matters of personal status, marriage, divorce, alimony, wills and probate, custody of children, paternity and adoption. Jewish divorce law is far more reasonable than the English law, and works simply, cheaply and expeditiously, but difficulties have frequently arisen over the marriage laws. There are no civil marriages in Israel. Thus a Jew who may want to marry a non-Jew cannot do so in Israel, nor may anyone who is a *Cohen*, that is, a descendant of the Jewish priesthood, marry a divorcée. When Supreme Court Justice Chaim Cohen wanted to do so he had to marry in New York, and a number of Aguda members of the Knesset wanted to have him unseated as a result.

(Utterances, perhaps even more than actions, can rouse the religious parties. When Ben Gurion, an inveterate Bible scholar, once queried the scriptural account of the Exodus, the Aguda tabled a motion of censure in the Knesset and he had to explain that he had been speaking in his private capacity.)

But apart from the religious laws which are enforced by the public authorities, religious groups have sometimes taken the law into their own hands. Thus drivers who try to cross through certain areas of Jerusalem on the Sabbath risk a barrage of stones. These attacks have often been needlessly provoked, but on other occasions innocent travellers have been set upon, and there have been numerous clashes between zealots and police. There were running battles in the streets of Jerusalem in 1958, when zealots demonstrated against the opening of a mixed bathing pool as a 'desecration of the Holy City'.

The Aguda is not the Neturei Karta, and the Mizrachi and Hapoel Hamizrachi are not the Aguda, but all groups tend to be judged by their extreme elements, and those Israelis who might have been disposed to favour traditionalism have recoiled at the sight of traditionalists on the rampage.

The difficulty of the moderates like the Mizrachi is that they have always had to fight a war on two fronts against the ultras on the one hand and against the secularists on the other.

When Kalischer wrote *Drishat Zion* it was to convince his religious brethren that practical steps could be taken to restore Zion, and should be; but the majority remained unconvinced, and even those who were sufficiently inspired by his arguments to prepare themselves for Aliya did not explore the full implications of what Jewish statehood would mean in terms of Halacha (traditional Jewish law).

The Halacha, though having its source in the Torah, has been shaped by Jewish experience, and Jewish experience for the past two thousand years has been exilic. The Halacha has been conditioned by the anxiety of a harassed minority to preserve itself, and thus though it may make severe demands on its adherents one can live by it only so long as the outside society does not. The devout Jew living in the diaspora may maintain his traditional observances without difficulty, and he may do so in Israel by virtue of the fact that the majority of Israelis do not. In short, what the religious authorities are trying to do is to adapt a body of laws evolved for one situation to fit quite another.

So far it has not worked, and it does not look as if it ever can work, and religion, instead of being part of the broad front of progress, has been a petitioner, winning a concession here, extorting a privilege there, protesting, demanding, reconciled to eternal minority status. It is one thing to believe in the Kingdom of Heaven, but quite another to believe that the religious parties, as at present constituted, can make it manifest on earth.

(In recent years a number of Reform and Liberal congregations have been established in Israel, but they are colonial offshoots of American synagogual bodies, without indigenous roots. They have a minute following and are of no consequence, though they enjoy a certain sympathy because of the persecution they have suffered from the entrenched religious groups.)

Yet if Zionism is to continue to have an appeal one cannot see how it can be anything other than religious.

Nor can the Arabs' case that Israel has usurped their homeland be answered in anything other than religious terms. How else may one justify the annexation of the Old City of Jerusalem ?

Israel is in fact a religious state almost in spite of herself. The ruling parties may be dominated by secularists, but when the Wailing Wall was taken, Ben Gurion, who is about as much at home in a place of worship as a Bishop in a casino, went rushing to it, as did Moshe Dayan and Levi Eshkol. Here they were at the source of what it means to be a Jew, and what the Jewish state was about.

Nationalism is a waning force in the West and it will wane in Israel once she is secure in her frontiers.

Antisemitism will, perhaps, never be eradicated, but it is unlikely to become so virulent as to make Jews quiver in their suburbs. Already immigration to Israel depends on those who want to go rather than those who have to go.

One of the strongest instincts in the Jew is the desire to be among his fellows, a Jew among Jews, and it is fully met in Israel, but this feeling has been nourished by centuries of exclusion and one wonders how long it will remain.

The restless dynamism of Israel, its feeling that there are new social and economic frontiers to be conquered, is in itself appealing to the youthful imagination, but it is all part of Israel's own youthfulness, and the dynamism, given new life for a moment by the six days' war, is slowing down. Israel is not, and perhaps never has been, a country freely open to the talented, and the well-connected mediocrity will usually get preferment over the gifted maverick. And added to this is the holy awe accorded to seniority, or the *Vetek* system, as it is known. A veteran in office has the security of tenure of a High Court judge and can only be dislodged, or indeed, prevented from advancing, by high crimes and misdemeanours. Everybody awaits his turn. The second Aliya is only now beginning to die off (one does not retire in Israel) and the third is stepping forward. In short, the young man with an acute sense of purpose, anxious to get things done, can be as frustrated in Israel as anywhere else.

One returns to religion. The Zionist movement, aware that Judaism is the only dependable link between Israel and world

Jewry, and startled by the inroads of assimilation, has launched a network of Jewish day schools in the diaspora. The Israeli Government, for its part, has tried to inculcate an understanding of recent Jewish history in its schools, and an appreciation of Jewish tradition and practice. It has been helped by the excavations at Masada, the Dead Sea fortress which was the last redoubt of the Jewish rebels in the wars against Rome. Here was at once an epic of courage and zeal, and a reminder of the faith at the source of Jewish experience.

But the overall position has not changed. There has been no renaissance of faith in Israel, or anything like it, but a clinging to old ways of thought, and a reiteration of old precepts.

There is a passage in the Book of Micah which embodies the ultimate aspirations of religious Zionism.

> 'But in the end of days it shall come to pass,
> That the mountain of the Lord's house shall
>   be established at the top of the mountains,
> And it shall be exalted above the hills;
> And people shall flow into it.
> And many nations shall go and say: Come ye,
>   and let us go up to the mountain of the Lord,
> And to the house of the God of Jacob;
> And He will teach us His ways,
> And we will walk in His paths;
> For out of Zion shall go forth the law,
> And the word of the Lord from Jerusalem.'[64]

While there is the insistence that the ossified code inherited from exile is the true law, there can be no renaissance, nor any hope that the prophetic role of Zion will be fulfilled.

Notes on the text

1 Goodman, P., *History of the Jews*, London, 1939, p 63.
2 Parkes, J., *Antisemitism*, London, 1963, p 63.
3 Kalischer, Z.H., *Drishat Zion*.
4 BILU stems from the initial letters in the Hebrew of Isaiah ii. 5: *Beth Ya'acov Lecho V'nelcha*, 'O house of Jacob, come ye, let us go'.
5 Weizmann, C., *Trial and Error*, London, 1949, p 63.
6 George, L., *War Memoirs*, London, 1933, pp 586–7.
7 Weizmann, C., *Trial and Error*, p 191.
8 The most complete analysis of the Balfour Declaration is given in Stein, L., *The Balfour Declaration*, London, 1961.

9 Cohen, I., *A Short History of Zionism*, London, 1951, p 68.
10 Gurion, B., *The Jews in their Land*, London, 1966, p 295.
11 Louvish, M., unpublished manuscript.
12 Cohen, I., *History of Zionism*, p 90.
13 *White Paper*, Cmd. 1540.
14 *Churchill White Paper*, Cmd. 1700.
15 *Great Britain and Palestine, 1915–45*, a paper published by the Royal Institute of International Affairs, London, 1946. The currency under the Mandate was £P (Palestinian Pounds). Since 1948 it has been IL (Israeli Liroth).
16 *Observer*, 8 July 1934.

17 *White Paper*, Cmd. 5957.
18 *The Times*, 10 June 1936.
19 *White Paper*, Cmd. 1700.
20 *White Paper*, Cmd. 1785.

21 *White Paper*, Cmd. 3692.
22 *Shaw Report*, HMSO 58–9096.
23 *White Paper*, Cmd. 3692.
24 Weizmann, C., *Trial and Error*, p 413.
25 *The Times*, 14 February 1931.
26 *Great Britain and Palestine*, pp 57–8.
27 *Blue Book*, Cmd. 5479.
28 ibid.
29 Weizmann, C., *Trial and Error*, p 418.
30 *Palestine Partition Commission*, Cmd. 5854.
31 Sykes, C., *Cross Roads to Israel*, London, 1965, p 215.
32 *White Paper*, Cmd. 6019.
33 Sykes, C., *Cross Roads to Israel*, p 234.
34 Gurion, B., *The Jews in their Land*, p 237.

4 THE END OF THE MANDATE
35 Quoted by Sykes, C., *Cross Roads to Israel*, p 311.
36 *Memoirs of Cordell Hull*, London, 1948, pp 1534–5.
37 Crossman, R.H.S., *Palestine Mission*, London, 1947.
38 Truman, H.S., *Years of Trial and Hope*, London, 1955, pp 141–74.
39 Cohen, I., *A Short History of Zionism*, pp 190–1.
40 *The Times*, 9 September 1947.
41 Joseph, D., *The Faithful City*, New York, 1960, pp 70–105.
42 ibid., pp 161–89.

5 THE SINEWS OF STATEHOOD
43 *Facts about Israel*, Govt Press Office, Tel-Aviv, 1966, p 78.
44 ibid., pp 140–56.
45 ibid., pp 157–68.
46 Litvinoff, B., *Road to Jerusalem*, London, 1967, pp 37–56.
47 Kraines, O., *Government and Politics in Israel*, Cambridge, Mass., 1961, pp 137–61.
48 *Israel Government Year Book*, 1966, pp 290–7.

6 POLITICS AND PARLIAMENT
49 The Second Viscount Samuel.
50 Edelman, M., *Ben Gurion*, London, 1964, p 41.

51 Barer, S., *Magic Carpet*, London, 1952.
52 In 1949 Malben was established by the American Joint Distribution Committee, a Jewish philanthropic body, to deal with the old, the handicapped and the chronically sick. By the end of 1965 over 250,000 aged immigrants had passed through its hands, and it had spent $152,000,000 to help them.
53 Chaim Arlosoroff, the Political Secretary of the Jewish Agency, was murdered while strolling with his wife in Tel-Aviv in 1933. A revisionist extremist was arrested and charged, but released for lack of evidence.

8 SINAI AND AFTER

54 Sir Anthony Eden in his Guildhall speech.
55 Published in *Israel Year Book*, Jewish Agency, Jerusalem, 1966.

10 THE LAND AND THE PEOPLE

56 Joshua xii. 14.

11 THE ECONOMY

57 Horowitz, D., *The Economics of Israel*, London, 1967, p 6.
58 Rubner, A., 'The Priceless Land of Israel', *Land Economics*, November, 1958.
59 *Government Year Book*, 1966, p 49.
60 *Israel Year Book*, 1966.

13 THE ARAB MINORITY

61 *Facts about Israel*, 1966, pp 57–9.
62 Schwarz, W., *The Arabs in Israel*, London, 1959, p 106.
63 ibid., pp 83–96.

POSTSCRIPT

64 Micah iv. 1–3.

Glossary

AGUDAS YISRAEL   (known also as the AGUDA.) Association of Israel. Right-wing, ultra religious party.

ALIYA   Immigration. Often used to refer to a wave of immigrants, as in the First Aliya, the Second Aliya, etc.

ASSEPHAT HANIVCHARIM   The elected assembly of the Jewish community in Palestine (the Yishuv) during the Mandate.

BETHAR   Youth movement of the Revisionist Party.

BILU   Spearhead group of the Chovevei Zion (see below) who were among the first of the pioneers to settle in Palestine at the end of the last century.

BRIT-SHALOM   Covenant of Peace. Group founded by Dr Judah Magnes for Arab-Jewish understanding and the creation of a bi-national state in Palestine.

CHOVEVEI ZION   Lovers of Zion. A movement which began in Russia and gradually spread throughout Europe for the settlement of Jews in Palestine. It preceded the foundation of the Zionist organization by Herzl, and eventually merged with it.

GAHAL   The political bloc formed in 1965 through the fusion of the Herut and Liberal party.

HAGANA   The Jewish underground army.

HALUKA   The distribution of alms.

HAVLAGA   Restraint.

200

HASHOMER   The self-defence units formed by the first Jewish settlers.

HASHOMER HATZAIR   The Young Watchmen. A Marxist socialist group which is particularly strong in the kibbutzim and which is the mainstay of Mapam (see below).

HASKALA   Enlightenment. A movement, originating in eighteenth-century Germany, to break away from the narrow limits of Jewish life and acquire the culture and customs of the outside world.

HAPOEL HAMIZRACHI   The Mizrach Worker. Religious party, moderately left-wing, moderately orthodox. In 1956 it joined with Mizrachi to form the National Religious Party.

HERUT   The Freedom Party. Extreme right-wing political group, a successor to the Revisionist Party, founded by Menahem Beigin. It is now part of Gahal.

HEVRAT OVDIM   The holding company of the various Histadrut enterprises (see below).

HISTADRUT   The Federation of Labour, which is Israel's TUC as well as a cooperative organization controlling a distribution network and numerous economic enterprises directed through the Hevrat Ovdim.

IRGUN TZVAI LEUMI   The National Military Society. Right-wing terrorist group led by Menachem Beigin which flourished during the last days of the Mandate.

KEREN HAYESOD   A fund established by the Zionist Organization in 1920 for the development of a Jewish national home in Palestine and which continues to attract large sums from Jewish communities throughout the world.

KIBBUTZ   Collective settlement.

KNESSET   The Assembly. Israel's House of Commons (there is no upper house).

KOL YISRAEL   The Voice of Israel. The national broadcasting service.

MAPAI The Israel Workers' Party. The largest party in Israel, moderate, left-wing, which has been at the centre of every coalition since the creation of the state.

MAPAM The United Workers' Party. It stands well to the left of Mapai and is strongly represented in the kibbutzim.

MIZRACHI Right-wing partner of Hapoel Hamizrachi in the National Religious Party.

MOSHAV Cooperative Settlement.

NAHAL Pioneering Fighting Youth. Young recruits who spend part of their military service as agricultural workers in front-line settlements.

PALMACH The spearhead of the Hagana.

POALEI AGUDAS YISRAEL The Aguda Workers of Israel. Left-wing, ultra religious. Stands to Aguda approximately as the Hapoel Hamizrachi stands to Mizrachi, though the two are not united in one party.

VAAD LEUMI The National Council. The executive arm of the Assephat Hanivcharim.

VEIDA Conference.

YISHUV The Jewish community in Palestine.

Who's Who

ADLER, Emil (b. Czechoslovakia 1900). Professor of Physical Medicine, Hebrew University. Head of Department of Physical Medicine Hadassah Hospital. Educated at German University, Prague and the Universities of Vienna and Breslau. Settled in Palestine 1939.

ADLER, Matityahu (b. Czechoslovakia 1920). Director General Bar-Ilan University. Educated at Hebrew University. Police Inspector 1944–7. Former Mayor of Beersheba.

ADLER, Saul Aron (b. 1895). Educated at the University of Leeds and School of Tropical Medicine, Liverpool. Parasitologist at the Hebrew University, Jerusalem.

ALTERMAN, Nathan (b. Poland 1910). Hebrew poet. Settled in Palestine 1925. On the staff of *Haaretz* 1934–43.

AGNON, Shmuel Yosef (b. Buczacz, Galicia 1888). Nobel Prize winner for literature, 1966. Came to Palestine with the Second Aliya in 1907. Worked for a period in Germany, but has lived in Jerusalem since 1924. His numerous works, some of which have been translated in over a dozen languages, include *We-haya-he-Akov le-Moshor* ('And the Bent Shall Become Straight'), *Etmol Shilshom* ('Yesterday and the Day Before'), and *Oreach Nata Lalun* ('A Guest Stays the Night'), and 'Days of Awe', an anthology of Jewish legends and apophthegms surrounding the New Year and the Day of Atonement.

AGZIN, Benjamin (b. Latvia 1904). Professor of Political Science and Constitutional Law, Hebrew University. Educated at Universities of Vienna, Paris, Harvard. Director American Zionist Emergency Council 1945–7. Settled in Israel 1949.

AGRANAT, Simon (b. USA 1906). President, Supreme Court. Educated at Chicago University. Settled in Palestine in 1930 and was a magistrate from 1940 to 1948. In 1948 he was appointed President of the Haifa District Court, and was elevated to the Supreme Court two years later.

ALLON, Yigal. Brigadier General (b. 1918). Educated at the Hebrew University and St Antony's College, Oxford. Served as a Palmach commander during the war and was C./in/C. from 1945 until the War of Liberation. Directed operation Horeb which drove Egyptians from Israel. Member of Kibbutz Genossar, and a former Secretary General of Ahdut Avoda. He was elected to the Knesset in 1955 and has been Minister of Labour since 1961.

ALMOGI, Joseph (b. 1910). Settled in Palestine 1930. Member of Hagana command 1933–9. Prisoner of war in Germany 1941–5. General Secretary Haifa Labour Council 1945–59, and Secretary General of Mapai 1959–62. Former Minister of Housing and Development.

ARANNE, Zalman (b. Russia 1899). Minister of Education and Culture. Educated at the University of Kharkov. Secretary General of Mapai 1948–52. Entered the Knesset in 1949.

AVIDAR, Yosef. Brigadier General (b. 1906). Diplomat. Came to Palestine with Third Aliya. Member of Hagana High Command from 1937 to 1946 and was specially concerned with the supply of military equipment.

AVRIEL, Ehud (b. 1917). Diplomat, who negotiated the crucial Czech arms deal during the War of Liberation. Served variously as Minister to Czecho/slovakia, Hungary and Romania, from 1948 to 1950, and Ambassador to Ghana, Liberia and the Congo. Director General of the Prime Minister's Office from 1951 to 1957. Ambassador to Italy 1967.

BARKATT, Reuven (b. 1906). Diplomat. Educated at the Universities of Strasbourg and Paris. Settled in Palestine in 1926. One time Director of the Political Department of the Histadrut; Ambassador to Norway 1960–1; Secretary General of Mapai 1962–6.

BAR/YEHUDA, Israel (b. Russia 1895). Settled in Palestine in 1926. Leading figure in the Ahdut Avoda Party. Member of Kibbutz Yagur. Minister of the Interior 1955–9; Minister of Transport 1962–5.

BARZILAI, Israel (b. Poland 1913). Minister of Health. Settled in Palestine 1934. Member of Kibbutz Negba. Political Secretary of Mapam 1953–5.

BECKER, Ahron (b. 1906). Settled in Palestine in 1924. Member of Mapai Secretariat. Secretary General of the Histadrut.

BEIGIN, Menachem (b. 1913). Founder of the Herut Party, and head of the Irgun Tzvai Leumi from 1943 until it was disbanded five years later. Educated Warsaw University. Head of Betar, the Revisionist Youth Movement, in Czechoslovakia and Poland. Arrested by Russians in 1940 and spent two years in Siberian labour camp. Arrived with Polish army in Palestine in 1942. Member of the Knesset. Resigned from the chairmanship of Herut in 1966.

BEN-AMI, Oved (b. Palestine 1905). Chairman, Board of Directors Kupat Am Bank. Founder and former Mayor of Nathanya. Co-founder of *Maariv*, Israel's daily paper. Founder of Israel's Diamond Cutting Industry.

BENDOR, Shumel (b. Belfast 1909). Deputy-Director-General Prime Minister's Office. Educated Liverpool University. Settled in Palestine in 1932. Became Vice-Principal, Reali School, Haifa. Wing-Commander Israel Air Force 1948. Head of US Department of Foreign Office, and held diplomatic office as Minister to Prague, 1957–9; Bucharest 1959–61. Head of the West European Department of Foreign Office, 1961–3.

BEN GURION, Amos (b. London 1920). Son of David Ben Gurion. General Manager ATA Textiles. Major in the British Army during the Second World War. Former Commander Tel-Aviv District Israel Police.

BEN GURION, David. See pp 91–2.

BEN-HAIM, Paul (b. 1897). Israel's leading composer. Settled in Palestine 1933, after serving as pianist and conductor in various German cities. Director New Jerusalem Academy of Music 1949–54. Hon. President Israel Composers Association. Awarded Israel State Prize in 1957 for symphonic work *The Sweet Psalmist of Israel*.

BEN-NATAN, Asher (b. Austria 1921). Ambassador to Germany. Educated Geneva University. Settled in Palestine 1938. Former Secretary Kibbutz Medorot-Zeraim.

BENTOV, Mordechai (b. 1900). Journalist and politician. Founder of the Mapam daily *Al Hamishmar*. Member of Mapam Secretariat. Minister of Labour in Provisional government. Minister of Development, 1955–61.

BENTSUR, Shmuel (b. 1906). Israel Ambassador to Switzerland. Head of East European Division of Foreign Office 1952–6; Deputy Director General 1958–62.

BERENBLUM, Isaac (b. 1903). Pathologist. Professor of Cancer Research the Weizmann Institute since 1962. Educated at Leeds University. Director Oxford University Research Centre of British Empire Cancer Campaign, 1940–8. Visiting Professor of Oncology, Hebrew University 1950–6.

BERGMAN, David Ernst (b. Germany 1903). Professor of Organic Chemistry Hebrew University. Educated Berlin University. Settled in Palestine 1934. Chairman of Atomic Energy Commission and Director of Research Ministry of Defence until 1966.

BERGMAN, Samuel Hugo, Professor (b. 1883). Rector of Hebrew University 1935–8. Dean of the Faculty of Humanities 1952–3. Member *Institut International de Philosophie*. His numerous works include: *The Philosophy of Kant* (1927); *The Philosophy of Maimon* (1932); *God and Man in Modern Thought* (1956), and *Faith and Reason* (1961).

BERINSON, Zvi (b. 1907). Supreme Court Justice. Educated Jesus College, Cambridge. Legal Adviser to Histadrut 1936–49. Director General Ministry of Labour 1949–53. Member of Supreme Court since 1954.

BERNSTEIN, Peretz (b. 1890). Former President of the General Zionist Party, and former head of the now defunct General Zionist daily *Haboker*. Minister of Trade Industry and Commerce in Provisional government, and Minister of Commerce and Industry from 1952 to 1955. His party has been a difficult partner in a coalition and he has in recent years attempted to form an effective right-wing opposition party. In 1961 he became head of the Liberal Party which resulted from the fusion of the General Zionists and the Progressives.

BUBER, Martin (1878–1965). Philosopher. Professor of Science of Religion, University of Frankfurt. Settled in Palestine in 1933. Professor of Social Philosophy at Hebrew University. The best known of his many works are

206

perhaps: *Tales of the Hasidim* (1947); *Between Man and Man* (1946); *Israel and the World* (1948); *The Prophetic Faith* (1949); *Eclipse of God* (1952); *Elija* (1963).

BURG, Yosef (b. 1909). Minister of Social Welfare since 1959. Member of the Hapoel Hamizrachi (left-wing faction of the National Religious Party). Educated at the Universities of Berlin and Leipzig, the Berlin Rabbinical Seminary, and the Hebrew University. Deputy Speaker in the first Knesset; Minister of Health 1951–2; Minister of Posts and Telegraphs 1952–8.

CARMEL, Moshe (b. 1911). Minister of Transport and Communications. Settled in Palestine in 1924. Educated at the Hebrew University and the Sorbonne. Member of Kibbutz Na'an. Former member of the Haganah High Command. Commander of the Northern front in the War of Liberation. Leader of the Ahdut Avoda faction in the Alignment.

COHEN, Chaim (b. 1911). Supreme Court Justice. Educated at the Universities of Munich and Hamburg, and Hebrew University. Minister of Justice and Acting Attorney General 1952; Attorney General, 1952–60, and in Supreme Court since. He has been at the centre of controversy after marrying a divorcée in defiance of Jewish traditional law, and attempts have been made by ultra-religious groups to unseat him.

COMAY, Michael (b. Capetown 1908). Permanent Representative at UN since 1960. Major in South African army 1940–5. On political staff of Jewish Agency 1946–8. Ambassador to Canada 1953–7.

DAGAN, Avigdor (b. 1912). Minister to Yugoslavia. Educated Prague University. Ambassador to Poland 1962–4. Poet and novelist.

DAVID, Jean (b. Romania 1908). Painter. Educated Ecole des Beaux Arts, Paris. Escaped to Palestine in fishing boat 1942. Government adviser on industrial design 1949–51.

DAYAN, Moshe. Major General (b. Kibbutz Degania 1915). Former Minister of Agriculture (1959–64). Educated Hebrew University. Member of Moshav Nahalal. Fought under Orde Wingate. Joined Palmach and lost an eye in the operation against Vichy French in Syria. Brigade Commander Jerusalem area during siege. Led Israel Delegation to the Rhodes armistice talks. Chief of Staff 1953–8. Directed Sinai campaign 1956. Appointed Minister of Defence, June 1967.

DE SHALIT, Amos (b. 1926). Physicist. Educated Hebrew University, and Swiss Federal Institute of Technology. Former Head of Nuclear Physics Department Weizmann Institute. Scientific Director of Weizmann Institute since 1961.

DE SHALIT, Meir (b. 1921). Director-General Israel Government Tourist Corporation.

DINUR, Benzion (b. 1884). Historian. Educated Universities of Berlin and Berne. Settled in Palestine 1921. Former head of Faculty of Humanities Hebrew University. Minister of Education and Culture 1951–5.

DISSENTSHIK, Arie (b. Latvia 1907). Editor of *Maariv*. Educated Vienna University. Settled in Palestine 1934. Editor of the General Zionist daily *Haboker* 1936–42.

DOBKIN, Eliahu (b. 1898). Head of the Youth Department of the Jewish Agency. Educated Kharkov University. Founded Hechalutz, the Jewish pioneer youth movement, in 1920.

DORI, Ya'akov. Major-General (b. 1899). President of the Haifa Technion 1951–66. Educated University of Ghent. Engineer. Helped to build and equip Hagana. Served in the Jewish Battalion in the First World War. Chief of Staff Hagana 1939–41; Chief of Staff Israel Army 1948–50.

EBAN, Abba (b. Capetown 1915). Foreign Minister. Educated at Cambridge University. Permanent Representative at UN 1949–59; Ambassador to USA 1950–9; Minister of Education and Culture 1960–3. President Weizmann Institute. One of the few Mapai figures to have risen to high office without having come up through the Histadrut machine.

ELATH, Eliahu (b. 1903). Diplomatist. Educated Hebrew University, and American University, Beirut. Ambassador to USA 1948–50; Ambassador to Britain 1952–9. President Hebrew University.

ESHEL, Arye (b. 1912). Educated Berlin University. Diplomatist. Settled in Palestine 1934. Served as Ambassador to Uruguay and later Brazil. Head of Latin American Department of the Foreign Office.

208

ESHKOL, Levi. See p. 119.

EYTAN, Walter (b. Munich 1910). Ambassador to France. Educated St Paul's School and Queen's College, Oxford. Director General of Foreign Office, 1948–59.

FEDERMAN, Samuel (b. Germany 1916). Hotelier. Managing Director of the Dan Hotel Corporation, Israel's biggest hotel chain. Chairman Israel Hotel Association.

FEINBERG, Nathan (b. 1895). Professor of International Law and International Relations, Hebrew University. Educated Zurich University and Graduate Institute of International Studies, Geneva. Head of Department of Ministry of Jewish Affairs, Lithuania, 1919–21. Settled in Palestine 1924.

FOERDOR, Yeshayahu Herbert (b. 1901). Chairman of Board of Directors of Bank Leumi and on board of numerous other banks and investment companies. Educated at the Universities of Heidelberg, Königsberg and Freiburg. Lawyer. Settled in Palestine in 1932. Managing Director of Rassco (Rural and Sub-urban Settlement Company) 1932–57. Member of the Knesset (Progressives) 1949–57.

FRAENKEL, Abraham Adolf. Professor (b. 1891). Mathematician. Rector Hebrew University 1938–40. Professor of Mathematics since 1931.

GALILI, Israel (b. 1911). Minister without Portfolio. Settled in Palestine in 1914. Member of Kibbutz Na'an. Former Secretary General Ahdut Avoda. Former Member of the Hagana High Command.

GVATI, Chaim (b. Russia 1901). Minister of Agriculture. Settled in Palestine 1924. Member Kibbutz Yitaf. Former Director General Ministry of Agri-culture.

GOLDMANN, Nahum (b. Poland 1895). President of the World Zionist Organization. Educated Universities of Heidelberg, Berlin and Marburg. Editor German Hebrew Encyclopedia. Left Germany, 1934. Jewish Agency Representative at League of Nations. Now resident in New York. Involved in bringing the General Zionist and Progressive together into the Liberal Party. His failure to settle in Israel has brought him under frequent attack from Ben Gurion. As head of the Zionist movement and President of the World Jewish Congress, he tends to function as Ambassador at Large for the Jewish people.

GOVRIN, Akiva (b. 1902). Settled in Palestine 1922. Chairman Mapai Parliamentary Party. Former Minister without Portfolio.

HAKIM, George (b. 1908). Archbishop of Acre and Galilee.

HALEVI, Benjamin (b. Germany 1910). Supreme Court Justice. Educated Berlin University. Settled in Palestine 1933.

HALEVY, Moshe (b. 1895). Theatrical producer. Actor and producer Habima Theatre, Moscow, 1918–25. Founder Ohel Theatre 1925.

HARMAN, Avraham (b. London 1914). Ambassador to USA. Educated Oxford University. Settled in Palestine 1938.

HAUSNER, Gideon (b. Poland 1915). Former Attorney General. Chief Prosecutor in Eichmann trial. Settled in Palestine 1927.

HAZAZ, Haim (b. Russia 1898). Novelist. Settled in Palestine 1931. His works (some of which have been adapted for the stage) have won him numerous awards including the Bialik Prize in 1942.

HERZOG, Jacob (b. Dublin 1921). Director-General Prime Minister's Office. Educated London University and Hebrew University. Settled in Palestine 1939. Former Ambassador to Canada.

HOROWITZ, David (b. 1899). Governor of the Bank of Israel. Educated at Universities of Vienna and Lvov. Secretary American Economic Committee for Palestine 1932–5 in which capacity he directed the flow of American investment in Palestine. Director General Ministry of Finance 1948–52. Author of numerous economic studies, including: *Jewish Colonization in Palestine* (1937); *Prediction and Reality in Palestine* (1945), and *State in the Making* (1953).

JOSEPH, Dov (b. Montreal 1899). Military Governor of Jerusalem during the 1948 siege. Educated McGill University and London University. Lawyer. Settled in Palestine in 1921. Treasurer and member of the Executive of the Jewish Agency. Arrested with Shertok and other members of the Executive in June 1946. Has held various portfolios in Israel government, including Supply, Agriculture, Communications, Commerce, Health and, latterly, Justice.

KAHANAMAN, Joseph (b. Lithuania 1888). Rabbi. Deputy in Lithuanian parliament. Head of Ponevetz Yehiva, which is perhaps the leading institution of its type in Israel. He is, apart from the authority he enjoys as head of Ponevetz, one of the most revered religious figures in Israel.

KATCHALSKY, Aharon (b. 1913). Educated Hebrew University. Head of Polymer Department of Weizmann Institute since 1947. Visiting Professor of Physical Chemistry Hebrew University since 1951.

KATZ, Mindru (b. Romania 1925). Educated Bucharest Academy of Music. Concert pianist. Settled in Israel 1959.

KHOUSHI, Abba (b. Poland 1898). Mayor of Haifa. Settled in Palestine 1920. Secretary General Mapai Workers' Council, 1938–51. Mapai member of Knesset 1949–51.

KISTER, Isaac (b. Poland 1905). Supreme Court Justice. Educated Lvov University. Settled in Palestine 1935. Tel-Aviv Magistrate 1945–8. District Judge 1949–65.

KOL, Moshe (b. Russia 1911). Minister of Tourism. Educated Hebrew University. Settled in Palestine 1932. Chairman of the Executive of the Liberal Party. Former head of the Youth Aliya Department of the Jewish Agency.

KOLLEK, Teddy (b. Vienna 1911). Mayor of Jerusalem. Settled in Palestine 1934. Founder member of Kibbutz Ein Gev. Since 1938 has been executive at large on one public mission after another. Sent to USA on behalf of Hagana 1947–8. Director General of the Prime Minister's Office 1952–64; Chairman Government Tourist Corporation 1955–64. Chairman of the Board of the Israel Museum, Jerusalem.

KUBOVY, Aryeh Leon (b. 1896). Chairman of Yad Vashem, the memorial foundation to the Jewish Holocaust. Educated Universities of Brussels and Liège. Head of Rescue Department of World Jewish Congress during the Second World War. Settled in Israel 1948. Legal Adviser to Histadrut 1950–1. Ambassador to Argentine 1953–8.

LANDAU, Moshe (b. Danzig 1912). Educated London University. Supreme Court Justice since 1953. Settled in Palestine 1933. Presided at Eichmann trial.

LASKOV, Haim (b. 1919). Director General Israel Ports Authority. Educated St Antony's College, Oxford. Major in British Army. Commander Upper Galilee during War of Liberation. Commander of armoured corps in the Sinai campaign. Chief-of-Staff 1958–60.

LAVON, Pinchas (b. Poland 1904). Educated Lvov University. One of the founders of Gordonia, the Polish Zionist youth organization. Settled in Palestine in 1929 and moved up rapidly in the echelons of Mapai and the Histadrut. Minister of Agriculture 1950–2. Minister of Defence 1954–5. It was during this period that the security mishap occurred which led to his resignation and the long-drawn out 'Lavon Affair'. In 1956 he became Secretary General of the Histadrut but was ousted from the office by Ben Gurion in 1961.

LEVANON, Chaim (b. Poland 1899). Former Mayor of Tel-Aviv. Educated Cracow University. Chairman Central Committee of the Liberal Party. Founder of Tel-Aviv University.

LEVAVI, Arye (b. Russia 1912). Director General Foreign Office. Educated Heidelberg and Hebrew University. Settled in Palestine 1932. Ambassador to Argentine 1958–60.

LEWIN, Daniel (b. 1907). Educated in Germany, Switzerland and France. Director of Asian Division, Foreign Office. Former Ambassador to Burma.

LOURIE, Arthur (b. South Africa 1903). Assistant Director General, Foreign Office. Educated Universities of Cambridge, Capetown and Harvard. Ambassador to Canada 1957–9, to Britain 1961–5.

LUZ, Kaddish (b. Russia 1895). Speaker of the Knesset. Minister of Agriculture 1955–9. Member of Kibbutz Degania Beth.

MANNY, Elija (b. Hebron 1907). Supreme Court Justice. Educated Liverpool University. Called to the Bar Gray's Inn 1932.

MAZAR, Benjamin (b. Russia 1906). Archaeologist. Educated in Universities of Berlin and Giessen. Settled in Palestine 1929. Professor of Biblical History and Historical Geography of Palestine, Hebrew University. Former President and Rector of the University. Chairman Israel Exploration Society.

MEIR, Golda (b. Russia 1898). Family moved to USA. Settled in Palestine 1921 and joined Moshav Merhavia. Secretary Women's Labour Council of Histadrut 1928. Former head of Kupat Holim and of Political Department of the Histadrut, and of the Political Department of the Jewish Agency. Ambassador to Russia 1948–9. Minister of Labour 1952–6 and Foreign Affairs 1956–66. General Secretary of Mapai.

NAMIR, Mordechai (b. 1897). Mayor of Tel-Aviv. Director of the Statistical Department of the Histadrut 1929–36. General Secretary of the Histadrut 1951. Minister of Labour 1956–9.

NISSIM, Izhak (b. Baghdad 1896). Sephardi Chief Rabbi of Israel. Settled in Palestine 1925. President of Rabbinical High Court.

OLSHAN, Itzhak (b. Lithuania 1895). Former President Supreme Court. Educated London University. Settled in Palestine 1912. Served in Jewish Legion in the First World War.

PARTOS, Oedoen (b. 1907). Composer. Educated Budapest Academy of Music. Settled in Palestine 1938. Head of Music Faculty Tel-Aviv University.

PERES, Shimon (b. 1923). Secretary General Rafi Party. Educated Harvard. Settled in Palestine in 1934. Director General Ministry of Defence 1955–9. Deputy Minister of Defence 1959–65. Followed Ben Gurion out of Mapai 1965.

PINCUS, Louis Aryeh (b. South Africa 1912). Chairman of the Jewish Agency Executive. Educated University of Witwatersrand. Settled in Palestine 1948. Managing Director El Al 1949–57.

PINES, Dan (b. 1900). Journalist and author. Educated Universities of Moscow and Kharkov. Co-editor of the Histadrut daily *Davar*.

RACAH, Giulio (b. Italy 1909). Physicist. Educated Universities of Florence and Rome and Eidgenossische Technische Hochschule, Zurich. Professor of Theoretical Physics Hebrew University 1939–61. Former Rector of Hebrew University.

RAFAEL, Gideon (b. Germany 1913). Israel's permanent representative at the UN. Educated University of Berlin. Settled in Israel 1934. Former Ambassador to Belgium and the European Economic Community.

RATNER, Yochanan (b. 1891). Architect. Educated Karlsruhe Institute of Technology. Settled in Palestine 1923. Professor and Dean of the Faculty of Architecture Haifa Technion, 1939–61.

ROSEN, Pinhas Felix (b. 1887). Former Minister of Justice. Co-founder of Progressive Party. Educated at Universities of Freiburg and Berlin. President of German Zionist Federation 1920–3. Settled in Palestine 1931.

RUBIN, Reuben (b. 1893). Painter. Exhibited at Venice Biennale 1948, 1950, 1952. Works in Museum of Modern Art, NY and Musée d'Art Moderne, Paris. Minister to Romania 1948–50

SAHAR, Yehezkiel (b. 1907). Diplomatist. Former private secretary to Chaim Weizmann. Educated at the London School of Economics. Inspector General Israel Police 1949–58. Ambassador to Austria 1958–61.

SALZMAN, Pnina (b. 1923). Concert pianist. Educated at the Paris Conservatoire. Gave first concert at age of 12. Has performed since then all over the globe.

SAMBURSKY, Shumel (b. 1900). Physicist. Trained at Universities of Königsberg, Berlin and Utrecht. Former Dean of Faculty of Science, Hebrew University and Director Israel Research Council.

SAMUEL, Edwin Herbert, 2nd Viscount (b. 1898). Principal of Israel Institute of Public Administration. Journalist and author; educated at Balliol College, Oxford and Columbia University. Intelligence Officer GHQ Palestine 1917–19. Served with Palestine Administration from 1920 to 1948. Labour Peer. Succeeded his father in 1963.

SAPIR, Pinhas (b. Lithuania 1909). Minister of Finance. Settled in Palestine in 1929 and worked for a time as an agricultural labourer. Former Director General of Ministry of Defence, Finance, and Minister of Commerce and Industry.

SASSON, Eliahu (b. 1902). Minister of Police. Head of Arab Division Political Department Jewish Agency 1932–47. Head of Middle Eastern Department Foreign Office 1947–50. Ambassador to Italy (1956–60) and Switzerland (1960–1). Former Minister of Posts.

SHALTIEL, David (b. 1903). Ambassador to Holland. Educated University of Hamburg. Settled in Palestine 1923. Commander of Jerusalem region during War of Liberation. Former Inspector General Israel Army.

SHAPIRO, Haim Moshe (b. 1902). Minister of the Interior. Educated Berlin Rabbinical Seminary. Settled in Palestine 1925. Chairman of the Hapoel Hamizrachi faction of the National Religious Party.

SHAPIRO, Ya'acov Shimshon (b. Russia 1902). Minister of Justice. Educated Kharkov University Medical School and Jerusalem Law School. Settled in Palestine 1924. Founder member of Kibbutz Givat Hasholosha. Former Attorney General.

SHARETT, Moshe. See p. 104.

SHAZAR, Zalman. See p. 88.

SHINNAR, Felix Elieser (b. 1905). Co-head of delegation which negotiated Reparations Agreement with Germany. Head (with rank of Ambassador) of Israel mission to implement the Agreement. Educated Universities of Tubingen, Heidelberg and Frankfurt. Settled in Palestine 1934. Managing Director of Israel's leading daily, *Haaretz*, 1937–49. Chairman of Delek Fuel Corporation and Director of numerous other concerns.

SHITRIT, Bechor Shalom (1895–1966). Former Minister of Police. Joined Palestine police in 1922. Head of Police Training School 1929–35. Chief Magistrate Lydda 1935–48.

SHLONSKY, Abraham (b. 1900). Poet. Educated Sorbonne. Settled in Palestine 1921. Translator of Shakespeare and Pushkin into Hebrew.

SHRAGAI, Shlomo Zalman (b. Poland 1899). Mizrachi leader and ideologist. Founder of the Young Mizrachi movement in Poland. Came to Palestine with the Third Aliya in 1924. Worked for a time as a labourer. Became Chairman of Palestine Broadcasting Services in 1938. The first Mayor of Jerusalem (1950–2). Head of Immigration Department of the Jewish Agency.

SILBERG, Moshe (b. Lithuania 1900). Deputy President Supreme Court. Educated Universities of Marburg and Frankfurt-am-Main as well as in various

Talmudical schools. Settled in Palestine 1929. District Court Judge 1948 until raised to Supreme Court in 1950. Visiting Professor of Law of Personal Status, Hebrew University.

SIMON, Ernst (b. Germany 1899). Educationalist. Educated Universities of Berlin and Heidelberg. Professor of Education Hebrew University. Former Secretary of Brit-Shalom, which worked for Jewish-Arab cooperation. His numerous publications include *Bialik* (1935); *The Teaching of Pestalozzi* (1953), and *Martin Buber and German Jewry* (1958).

SNEH, Moshe (b. 1909). Chief editor *Kol Haam*, the Israel communist daily. Educated Free Polish University and University of Warsaw. Physician. Escaped to Palestine after the fall of Poland and became head of the Hagana. Directed Jewish Resistance Movement against Britain at the end of the War. Was forced to take refuge in France and from there organized illegal immigration. Member of the Political Committee of Mapam. In 1952, after the Mapam split he headed the left-wing group which joined the Communist Party.

SUSSMANN, Joel (b. Poland 1910). Supreme Court Justice. Educated Universities of Frankfurt, Heidelberg, Berlin and Cambridge. Appointed to Supreme Court, 1953.

TALMON, Yakov Leib (b. Poland 1916). Professor of Modern History Hebrew University. Visiting Fellow St Catherine's College, Oxford. His publications include *The Origins of Totalitarianism* and *Romanticism and Revolt*.

TEKOAH, Yosef (b. 1925). Former Ambassador to USSR. Educated Harvard University. Legal Adviser to Foreign Office 1949-53. Director of Armistice Affairs 1953-8.

TSUR, Ya'akov (b. 1906). Chairman Jewish National Fund. Educated Florence University, Sorbonne. Ambassador to France 1953-9.

UNTERMAN, Iser Yehuda (b. Poland 1886). Rabbi. Ashkenazi Chief Rabbi. Communal Rabbi of Liverpool 1923-46; Chief Rabbi of Tel-Aviv 1946-64.

WARHAFTIG, Zerach (b. Poland 1906). Minister of Religious Affairs. Educated Warsaw University. Lawyer. Vice-President Polish Mizrachi 1932-9. Vice President Hapoel Hamizrachi, USA 1943-7. Settled in Palestine 1957.

WEISGAL, Meyer Wolf (b. Poland 1894). Executive Chairman Weizmann Institute. Educated Columbia University. Journalist and administrator. Personal Political Representative of Chaim Weizmann in America, 1942–6.

WEITZ, Raanan (b. 1913). Agriculturist. Educated Hebrew University and University of Florence. Attached to Intelligence Corps, 8th Army in Second World War. Head of Agricultural Settlement Department, Jewish Agency.

WITKON, Alfred (b. 1910). Supreme Court Justice. Educated Universities of Bonn, Berlin and Freiburg. Called to the Bar Middle Temple 1936. President Jerusalem District Court 1948. Elevated to Supreme Court 1954.

YADIN, Yigael, General (b. 1917). Archaeologist. Leader of the Masada Expedition. Former Chief-of-Staff Israel Army. Educated Hebrew University. Professor of Archaeology at the University since 1963. His publications include: *The Message of the Scrolls* (1957); *Warfare in Biblical Lands* (1963), and *Masada* (1966).

YAHIL, Chaim (b. Czechoslovakia 1905). Head of the Israel Foundation for Cultural Relations with World Jewry. Educated in the Universities of Prague and Vienna. Settled in Palestine in 1929. Former Ambassador to Sweden and Director General of the Foreign Office.

ZADOK, Haim (b. Poland 1913). Minister of Trade and Industry.

Select Bibliography

British Government White Papers: HMSO Cmd. 1540: 1700: 3229: 3530: 3686: 6019

Antionius, G., *The Arab Awakening*, London, 1937
Bentwich, N., *Palestine*, London, 1934
Cohen, I., *The Zionist Movement*, London, 1951
Crossman, R.H.S., *Palestine Mission*, London, 1947
Edelman, M., *Ben Gurion*, London, 1964
Eytan, W., *The First Ten Years*, New York, 1958
de Gaury, S., *The New State of Israel*, London, 1952
Gurion, B. *The Jews in their Land*, London, 1966
Hertzeberg, A., ed., *The Zionist Idea*, New York, 1959
Horowitz, D., *The Economics of Israel*, London, 1967
Hyamson, A., *Palestine. A Policy*, London, 1942
Joseph, D., *The Faithful City*, New York, 1960
Kimche, J., *Seven Fallen Pillars*, London, 1950
Kirk, G., *A Short History of the Middle East*, London, 1957
Koestler, A., *Promise and Fulfilment*, London, 1949
Lawrence, T.E., *Revolt in the Desert*, London, 1927
Litvinoff, B., *Roads to Jerusalem*, London, 1967
Melchett, Lord, *Thy Neighbour*, London, 1936
Roth, C., *A Short History of the Jewish People*, London, 1935
Sacher, H., *The Establishment of a State*, London, 1967
Samuel, E., *Problems of Government in the State of Israel*, Jerusalem, 1956
Samuel, Viscount, *Memoirs*, London, 1945
Schwartz, W., *The Arabs in Israel*, 1959
Stein, L., *The Balfour Declaration*, London, 1961
Storrs, R., *Orientations*, London, 1937
Sykes, C., *Orde Wingate*, London, 1959; *Two Studies in Virtue*, London, 1953; *Cross Roads to Israel*, London, 1965
Viteles, H., *A History of the Cooperative Movement in Israel*, London, 1967
Weizmann, C., *Trial and Error*, London, 1949

Author's Acknowledgements

I wish to acknowledge my grateful thanks to Mr Naphtali Lau of *Haaretz*, Dr S. Levenberg, of the Jewish Agency, Mr Misha Louvish, Dr Nevil Mandel, and Mr Arie Peytan of the Israel Government Press Office, all of whom have in their different ways helped me in the preparation of this book, and none of whom may be in any way blamed for its shortcomings. I am grateful also to Mr D. P. Bower of Thames and Hudson, editor of this series, for a patience uncommon even in a British publisher.

C.B.

Picture Acknowledgements

Index

Numbers in italic refer to illustrations